50 Gut-Friendly Dish Recipes for Home

By: Kelly Johnson

Table of Contents

- Ginger Turmeric Carrot Soup
- Quinoa and Vegetable Stir-Fry
- Lemon Herb Baked Salmon
- Coconut Curry Lentil Stew
- Roasted Vegetable Salad with Lemon Dressing
- Zucchini Noodles with Pesto
- Grilled Chicken with Herbed Yogurt Sauce
- Mediterranean Chickpea Salad
- Miso-Glazed Cod
- Turkey and Vegetable Lettuce Wraps
- Cauliflower Rice Stir-Fry
- Spiced Lentil Soup
- Baked Sweet Potatoes with Chickpea Curry
- Greek Yogurt Chicken Skewers
- Eggplant Rollatini
- Spinach and Feta Stuffed Chicken Breast
- Shrimp and Avocado Salad
- Quinoa Stuffed Bell Peppers
- Roasted Brussels Sprouts with Balsamic Glaze
- Thai Coconut Chicken Soup
- Lemon Garlic Shrimp
- Baked Cod with Tomato and Olive Relish
- Butternut Squash and Kale Salad
- Turkey Meatballs in Tomato Sauce
- Roasted Cauliflower Tacos
- Lemon Rosemary Grilled Chicken
- Chickpea and Spinach Curry
- Asian Cabbage Salad
- Baked Falafel with Tahini Sauce
- Salmon Cakes with Dill Yogurt Sauce
- Lentil and Sweet Potato Shepherd's Pie
- Quinoa Tabouleh Salad
- Turkey Chili with Beans
- Ratatouille
- Coconut Lime Chicken Skewers

- Cucumber Noodle Salad with Peanut Dressing
- Spinach and Mushroom Quiche with Almond Flour Crust
- Baked Acorn Squash with Wild Rice Stuffing
- Lemon Herb Grilled Shrimp Skewers
- Black Bean and Sweet Potato Tacos
- Tomato Basil Zucchini Noodles
- Greek Chicken Souvlaki Bowls
- Cauliflower Pizza Crust with Veggie Toppings
- Roasted Beet and Arugula Salad
- Teriyaki Salmon with Steamed Broccoli
- Moroccan Spiced Chickpea Stew
- Turkey and Vegetable Skillet
- Eggplant and Tomato Casserole
- Coconut Curry Vegetable Soup
- Stuffed Bell Peppers with Ground Turkey and Quinoa

Ginger Turmeric Carrot Soup

Ingredients:

- 1 tablespoon olive oil or coconut oil
- 1 onion, chopped
- 3 cloves garlic, minced
- 1 tablespoon fresh ginger, grated
- 1 tablespoon fresh turmeric, grated (or 1 teaspoon ground turmeric)
- 1 lb (450g) carrots, peeled and chopped
- 4 cups (1 liter) vegetable broth or water
- Salt and pepper, to taste
- Coconut milk (optional, for garnish)
- Fresh cilantro or parsley, chopped (for garnish)

Instructions:

1. Prepare Ingredients: Peel and chop the onion, garlic, ginger, turmeric, and carrots.
2. Sauté Aromatics: In a large pot or Dutch oven, heat the olive oil over medium heat. Add the chopped onion and sauté until translucent, about 5 minutes. Add the minced garlic, grated ginger, and grated turmeric. Cook for another 1-2 minutes until fragrant.
3. Add Carrots: Add the chopped carrots to the pot and stir well with the aromatics.
4. Cook Soup: Pour in the vegetable broth or water to cover the vegetables. Bring to a boil, then reduce the heat to low. Cover and simmer for about 20-25 minutes or until the carrots are tender.
5. Blend Soup: Once the carrots are cooked through, remove the pot from the heat. Use an immersion blender to blend the soup until smooth and creamy. Alternatively, carefully transfer the soup in batches to a blender and blend until smooth.
6. Season: Season the soup with salt and pepper, adjusting to taste.
7. Serve: Ladle the soup into bowls. If desired, swirl in a spoonful of coconut milk for creaminess and garnish with chopped fresh cilantro or parsley.
8. Enjoy: Serve the ginger turmeric carrot soup hot and enjoy its comforting and soothing flavors.

This soup is not only delicious but also rich in antioxidants, vitamins, and anti-inflammatory properties from the ginger and turmeric. It's perfect for supporting gut health and overall well-being. Adjust the seasonings and consistency according to your preference. Pair it with some crusty bread or a side salad for a complete meal.

Quinoa and Vegetable Stir-Fry

Ingredients:

- 1 cup quinoa, rinsed
- 2 cups water or vegetable broth
- 2 tablespoons olive oil or coconut oil
- 1 onion, chopped
- 2 cloves garlic, minced
- 1 bell pepper (any color), sliced
- 1 zucchini, sliced
- 1 cup broccoli florets
- 1 cup snap peas or snow peas
- 1 carrot, sliced
- 1 tablespoon soy sauce or tamari (gluten-free option)
- 1 tablespoon rice vinegar
- 1 tablespoon sesame oil
- 1 teaspoon grated ginger
- Salt and pepper, to taste
- Optional toppings: chopped green onions, sesame seeds

Instructions:

1. Cook Quinoa: In a medium saucepan, combine the rinsed quinoa and water or vegetable broth. Bring to a boil, then reduce the heat to low. Cover and simmer for 15-20 minutes or until the quinoa is cooked and the liquid is absorbed. Remove from heat and let it sit, covered, for 5 minutes. Fluff with a fork.
2. Prepare Vegetables: While the quinoa is cooking, prepare the vegetables. Heat olive oil or coconut oil in a large skillet or wok over medium-high heat. Add the chopped onion and minced garlic. Sauté for 2-3 minutes until fragrant.
3. Add Vegetables: Add the sliced bell pepper, zucchini, broccoli florets, snap peas (or snow peas), and carrot to the skillet. Stir-fry for 5-7 minutes until the vegetables are tender-crisp but still vibrant.
4. Combine Quinoa and Vegetables: Add the cooked quinoa to the skillet with the vegetables. Stir well to combine.
5. Make Stir-Fry Sauce: In a small bowl, whisk together soy sauce or tamari, rice vinegar, sesame oil, grated ginger, salt, and pepper.
6. Finish Stir-Fry: Pour the stir-fry sauce over the quinoa and vegetables. Stir everything together until well coated and heated through, about 2-3 minutes.

7. Serve: Remove from heat. Taste and adjust seasoning if needed. Serve the quinoa and vegetable stir-fry hot, garnished with chopped green onions and sesame seeds if desired.
8. Enjoy: This quinoa and vegetable stir-fry is a complete and balanced meal on its own. It's packed with protein from quinoa and loaded with vitamins and fiber from the colorful vegetables. Enjoy this nutritious and gut-friendly dish for a satisfying lunch or dinner.

Feel free to customize this recipe by adding your favorite vegetables or protein sources such as tofu, chickpeas, or cooked chicken. It's versatile and can be adapted based on what you have on hand.

Lemon Herb Baked Salmon

Ingredients:

- 4 salmon fillets (about 6 ounces each), skin-on or skinless
- Salt and pepper, to taste
- 2 tablespoons olive oil
- 2 tablespoons fresh lemon juice
- 2 cloves garlic, minced
- 1 tablespoon fresh parsley, chopped
- 1 tablespoon fresh dill, chopped (or 1 teaspoon dried dill)
- 1 tablespoon fresh chives, chopped (optional)
- Lemon slices, for garnish
- Fresh herbs, for garnish

Instructions:

1. Preheat Oven: Preheat your oven to 375°F (190°C). Line a baking sheet with parchment paper or lightly grease with olive oil.
2. Prepare Salmon: Pat the salmon fillets dry with paper towels. Season both sides of the salmon fillets with salt and pepper.
3. Make Herb Mixture: In a small bowl, whisk together olive oil, lemon juice, minced garlic, chopped parsley, dill, and chives (if using).
4. Coat Salmon: Place the seasoned salmon fillets on the prepared baking sheet. Brush the herb mixture over the tops of the salmon fillets, ensuring they are evenly coated.
5. Bake Salmon: Bake the salmon in the preheated oven for about 12-15 minutes, or until the salmon is cooked through and flakes easily with a fork. Cooking time may vary depending on the thickness of the salmon fillets.
6. Garnish and Serve: Remove the baked salmon from the oven. Garnish with lemon slices and fresh herbs.
7. Serve: Serve the lemon herb baked salmon hot, alongside your favorite side dishes such as steamed vegetables, quinoa, or a fresh salad.
8. Enjoy: This lemon herb baked salmon is light, flavorful, and perfect for a healthy and satisfying meal. The combination of lemon and fresh herbs enhances the natural flavors of the salmon without overwhelming your digestive system.

Feel free to adjust the herbs and seasoning according to your taste preferences. You can also add a sprinkle of lemon zest for extra lemony flavor. This dish is not only delicious but also packed with nutrients that can support gut health and overall well-being.

Coconut Curry Lentil Stew

Ingredients:

- 1 tablespoon coconut oil or olive oil
- 1 onion, finely chopped
- 3 cloves garlic, minced
- 1 tablespoon fresh ginger, grated
- 1 red bell pepper, chopped
- 1 carrot, diced
- 1 cup dried brown lentils, rinsed
- 1 can (14 oz/400 ml) coconut milk
- 2 cups vegetable broth
- 2 tablespoons red curry paste
- 1 tablespoon soy sauce or tamari (gluten-free option)
- 1 tablespoon maple syrup or coconut sugar
- 1 teaspoon ground turmeric
- Salt and pepper, to taste
- Fresh cilantro, chopped (for garnish)
- Cooked rice or naan bread, for serving (optional)

Instructions:

1. Sauté Aromatics: In a large pot or Dutch oven, heat the coconut oil over medium heat. Add the chopped onion and sauté for 3-4 minutes until translucent.
2. Add Garlic and Ginger: Stir in the minced garlic and grated ginger. Cook for another 1-2 minutes until fragrant.
3. Add Vegetables: Add the chopped red bell pepper and diced carrot to the pot. Stir and cook for 5 minutes until the vegetables start to soften.
4. Add Lentils and Liquid: Add the rinsed brown lentils, coconut milk, and vegetable broth to the pot. Stir in the red curry paste, soy sauce or tamari, maple syrup or coconut sugar, and ground turmeric.
5. Simmer Stew: Bring the mixture to a boil, then reduce the heat to low. Cover and simmer for about 20-25 minutes, or until the lentils and vegetables are tender. Stir occasionally to prevent sticking.
6. Adjust Seasoning: Taste the stew and season with salt and pepper as needed.
7. Serve: Ladle the coconut curry lentil stew into bowls. Garnish with chopped fresh cilantro.
8. Enjoy: Serve the coconut curry lentil stew hot, either on its own or with cooked rice or naan bread for a complete and satisfying meal.

This coconut curry lentil stew is not only delicious and comforting but also packed with plant-based protein and fiber. The creamy coconut milk and aromatic spices create a flavorful base that's easy on the stomach and perfect for supporting gut health. Feel free to customize this recipe by adding your favorite vegetables or adjusting the level of spiciness according to your taste preferences.

Roasted Vegetable Salad with Lemon Dressing

Ingredients:

For the Salad:

- 2 cups mixed vegetables (such as bell peppers, zucchini, eggplant, cherry tomatoes, broccoli florets, or carrots), chopped into bite-sized pieces
- 2 tablespoons olive oil
- Salt and pepper, to taste
- Mixed salad greens (such as spinach, arugula, or lettuce)

For the Lemon Dressing:

- 1/4 cup olive oil
- Zest and juice of 1 lemon
- 1 garlic clove, minced
- 1 teaspoon Dijon mustard
- 1 tablespoon honey or maple syrup (optional, for sweetness)
- Salt and pepper, to taste

Optional Additions:

- Cooked quinoa or couscous
- Crumbled feta cheese or goat cheese
- Toasted nuts or seeds (such as pine nuts or pumpkin seeds)
- Fresh herbs (such as parsley or basil), chopped

Instructions:

1. Preheat Oven: Preheat your oven to 400°F (200°C).
2. Roast Vegetables: In a large mixing bowl, toss the chopped mixed vegetables with olive oil, salt, and pepper until evenly coated. Spread the vegetables in a single layer on a baking sheet lined with parchment paper.
3. Roast: Roast the vegetables in the preheated oven for about 20-25 minutes, or until they are tender and lightly browned. Stir halfway through cooking for even roasting.
4. Prepare Dressing: While the vegetables are roasting, prepare the lemon dressing. In a small bowl, whisk together the olive oil, lemon zest, lemon juice, minced

garlic, Dijon mustard, honey or maple syrup (if using), salt, and pepper until well combined. Adjust seasoning to taste.
5. Assemble Salad: In a large salad bowl, combine the mixed salad greens with the roasted vegetables. Toss gently to mix.
6. Add Extras: If desired, add cooked quinoa or couscous to the salad for added texture and protein. You can also sprinkle crumbled feta cheese or goat cheese, toasted nuts or seeds, and fresh herbs over the salad.
7. Drizzle Dressing: Drizzle the lemon dressing over the roasted vegetable salad and toss gently to coat everything evenly.
8. Serve: Serve the roasted vegetable salad with lemon dressing immediately as a satisfying and nutritious meal.

This roasted vegetable salad with lemon dressing is versatile and can be customized based on the vegetables and toppings you prefer. It's a great option for a light lunch or dinner, and the lemon dressing adds a refreshing and tangy flavor that complements the roasted vegetables perfectly. Enjoy this gut-friendly salad as a delicious and nourishing dish!

Zucchini Noodles with Pesto

Ingredients:

For the Zucchini Noodles:

- 4 medium zucchini
- Salt, to taste

For the Pesto:

- 2 cups fresh basil leaves, packed
- 1/2 cup pine nuts or walnuts
- 1/2 cup grated Parmesan cheese (optional, omit for dairy-free)
- 2 cloves garlic, peeled
- 1/2 cup extra-virgin olive oil
- Juice of 1 lemon
- Salt and pepper, to taste

Optional Toppings:

- Cherry tomatoes, halved
- Extra grated Parmesan cheese
- Fresh basil leaves, chopped
- Red pepper flakes (for a bit of heat)

Instructions:

1. Prepare Zucchini Noodles: Use a spiralizer or vegetable peeler to create zucchini noodles (zoodles) from the zucchini. If using a spiralizer, follow the manufacturer's instructions. If using a vegetable peeler, simply peel the zucchini lengthwise into thin strips. Place the zucchini noodles in a colander set over a bowl, sprinkle with salt, and let them sit for 10-15 minutes to release excess moisture. Then, pat dry with paper towels.
2. Make Pesto Sauce: In a food processor or blender, combine the basil leaves, pine nuts or walnuts, grated Parmesan cheese (if using), garlic cloves, and lemon juice. Pulse several times to chop the ingredients. With the food processor running, slowly drizzle in the olive oil until the pesto reaches a smooth and creamy consistency. Season with salt and pepper to taste.

3. Combine Zucchini Noodles with Pesto: In a large mixing bowl, toss the zucchini noodles with the freshly prepared pesto sauce until well coated.
4. Optional: Add Toppings: If desired, add cherry tomatoes, extra grated Parmesan cheese, chopped fresh basil leaves, and red pepper flakes to the zucchini noodles and toss gently.
5. Serve: Divide the zucchini noodles with pesto among serving plates or bowls. Garnish with additional toppings if desired.
6. Enjoy: Serve the zucchini noodles with pesto immediately as a light and flavorful meal. This dish is best enjoyed fresh and can be served cold or slightly warmed.

Zucchini noodles with pesto is a healthy and low-carb alternative to traditional pasta dishes. It's packed with nutrients and can be easily customized with your favorite toppings. This gut-friendly recipe is light on the stomach and perfect for those looking for a satisfying yet gentle meal. Enjoy the fresh flavors of basil and zucchini in this delightful dish!

Grilled Chicken with Herbed Yogurt Sauce

Ingredients:

For the Grilled Chicken:

- 4 boneless, skinless chicken breasts
- 2 tablespoons olive oil
- 2 cloves garlic, minced
- 1 teaspoon dried oregano
- 1 teaspoon dried thyme
- Salt and pepper, to taste

For the Herbed Yogurt Sauce:

- 1 cup plain Greek yogurt
- 2 tablespoons fresh lemon juice
- 2 tablespoons fresh parsley, chopped
- 1 tablespoon fresh dill, chopped
- 1 tablespoon fresh chives, chopped
- Salt and pepper, to taste

Optional Garnish:

- Lemon wedges
- Fresh herbs (parsley, dill, or chives), chopped

Instructions:

1. Marinate Chicken: In a bowl, combine olive oil, minced garlic, dried oregano, dried thyme, salt, and pepper. Place the chicken breasts in a shallow dish or resealable plastic bag, and pour the marinade over the chicken. Ensure the chicken is evenly coated with the marinade. Cover or seal the bag and refrigerate for at least 30 minutes (or up to 4 hours) to allow the flavors to meld.
2. Preheat Grill: Preheat your grill or grill pan to medium-high heat.
3. Grill Chicken: Remove the chicken breasts from the marinade and discard any excess marinade. Grill the chicken breasts for about 6-8 minutes per side, or until the internal temperature reaches 165°F (75°C) and the chicken is cooked through with beautiful grill marks. Cooking time may vary depending on the thickness of

the chicken breasts. Remove from the grill and let rest for a few minutes before serving.
4. Make Herbed Yogurt Sauce: While the chicken is grilling, prepare the herbed yogurt sauce. In a bowl, combine the plain Greek yogurt, fresh lemon juice, chopped parsley, chopped dill, chopped chives, salt, and pepper. Mix well until all ingredients are incorporated.
5. Serve: Slice the grilled chicken breasts and serve them with a generous dollop of herbed yogurt sauce on top. Garnish with lemon wedges and additional chopped fresh herbs, if desired.
6. Enjoy: Serve the grilled chicken with herbed yogurt sauce alongside your favorite side dishes such as roasted vegetables, salad, or rice. The herbed yogurt sauce adds a creamy and tangy flavor to the grilled chicken, making it a delightful and satisfying meal.

This grilled chicken with herbed yogurt sauce is not only delicious but also gut-friendly and packed with protein. It's a versatile dish that can be enjoyed for lunch or dinner, and the herbed yogurt sauce can be used as a dip or dressing for other dishes as well. Enjoy this flavorful and nourishing meal!

Mediterranean Chickpea Salad

Ingredients:

For the Salad:

- 2 cans (15 oz each) chickpeas (garbanzo beans), drained and rinsed
- 1 cucumber, diced
- 1 bell pepper (any color), diced
- 1 pint cherry tomatoes, halved
- 1/2 red onion, finely chopped
- 1/4 cup Kalamata olives, sliced
- 1/4 cup crumbled feta cheese (optional, omit for dairy-free)
- Fresh parsley, chopped (for garnish)
- Salt and pepper, to taste

For the Dressing:

- 1/4 cup extra-virgin olive oil
- 2 tablespoons red wine vinegar or lemon juice
- 1 clove garlic, minced
- 1 teaspoon dried oregano
- Salt and pepper, to taste

Instructions:

1. Prepare Chickpeas and Vegetables: In a large mixing bowl, combine the drained and rinsed chickpeas, diced cucumber, diced bell pepper, halved cherry tomatoes, chopped red onion, sliced Kalamata olives, and crumbled feta cheese (if using).
2. Make Dressing: In a small bowl or jar, whisk together the extra-virgin olive oil, red wine vinegar or lemon juice, minced garlic, dried oregano, salt, and pepper. Adjust seasoning to taste.
3. Combine Salad and Dressing: Pour the dressing over the chickpea and vegetable mixture. Toss gently to coat everything evenly with the dressing.
4. Chill (Optional): For optimal flavor, cover the salad and refrigerate for at least 30 minutes to allow the flavors to meld together. This step is optional but recommended.
5. Garnish and Serve: Before serving, sprinkle chopped fresh parsley over the salad as a garnish.

6. Enjoy: Serve the Mediterranean chickpea salad as a light and refreshing meal or side dish. It's perfect for picnics, potlucks, or as a healthy lunch option.

This Mediterranean chickpea salad is packed with fiber, protein, vitamins, and minerals from the chickpeas and fresh vegetables. The tangy and flavorful dressing enhances the natural flavors of the ingredients. Feel free to customize this salad by adding or substituting ingredients based on your preferences. You can also serve it with crusty bread or alongside grilled chicken or fish for a complete and satisfying meal. Enjoy this delicious and gut-friendly Mediterranean-inspired dish!

Miso-Glazed Cod

Ingredients:

- 4 cod fillets (about 6 ounces each), skinless
- 3 tablespoons white miso paste
- 2 tablespoons mirin (Japanese sweet rice wine)
- 1 tablespoon soy sauce or tamari (gluten-free option)
- 1 tablespoon honey or maple syrup
- 1 tablespoon rice vinegar
- 2 cloves garlic, minced
- 1 tablespoon grated fresh ginger
- Sesame seeds, for garnish
- Sliced green onions, for garnish
- Cooked rice or steamed vegetables, for serving (optional)

Instructions:

1. Preheat Oven: Preheat your oven to 400°F (200°C).
2. Make Miso Glaze: In a bowl, combine the white miso paste, mirin, soy sauce or tamari, honey or maple syrup, rice vinegar, minced garlic, and grated ginger. Mix well until smooth and combined.
3. Prepare Cod Fillets: Pat dry the cod fillets with paper towels. Place the cod fillets in a baking dish or on a baking sheet lined with parchment paper.
4. Apply Miso Glaze: Spoon the miso glaze over the cod fillets, spreading it evenly to coat each fillet.
5. Bake Cod: Bake the cod fillets in the preheated oven for about 12-15 minutes, or until the fish is cooked through and flakes easily with a fork.
6. Broil (Optional): If desired, turn on the broiler for the last 1-2 minutes of cooking to lightly brown and caramelize the miso glaze on top of the cod fillets.
7. Garnish and Serve: Remove the baked cod fillets from the oven. Sprinkle with sesame seeds and sliced green onions for garnish.
8. Serve: Serve the miso-glazed cod hot, accompanied by cooked rice or steamed vegetables if desired.
9. Enjoy: Enjoy this flavorful and tender miso-glazed cod as a healthy and satisfying meal. The combination of sweet, salty, and umami flavors from the miso glaze complements the delicate flavor of the cod perfectly.

This miso-glazed cod recipe is simple yet impressive, making it a great option for weeknight dinners or special occasions. It's a light and nutritious dish that's easy on the stomach and packed with protein. Serve with your favorite side dishes to complete the meal. Enjoy!

Turkey and Vegetable Lettuce Wraps

Ingredients:

For the Turkey Filling:

- 1 tablespoon olive oil
- 1 pound ground turkey (or chicken)
- 1 onion, finely chopped
- 2 cloves garlic, minced
- 1 red bell pepper, finely chopped
- 1 zucchini, finely chopped
- 1 carrot, grated
- 1 tablespoon soy sauce or tamari (gluten-free option)
- 1 tablespoon hoisin sauce
- 1 teaspoon sesame oil
- Salt and pepper, to taste
- Butter lettuce leaves (or iceberg lettuce), for wrapping

For Garnish (optional):

- Sliced green onions
- Chopped fresh cilantro
- Sesame seeds

Instructions:

1. Prepare Turkey Filling: Heat olive oil in a large skillet or wok over medium-high heat. Add the ground turkey and cook, breaking it up with a spoon, until browned and cooked through.
2. Add Vegetables: Add the chopped onion, minced garlic, and red bell pepper to the skillet with the turkey. Stir-fry for 2-3 minutes until the vegetables start to soften.
3. Add Zucchini and Carrot: Add the chopped zucchini and grated carrot to the skillet. Continue to stir-fry for another 3-4 minutes until all vegetables are tender.
4. Season the Filling: Stir in soy sauce or tamari, hoisin sauce, sesame oil, salt, and pepper. Cook for an additional 1-2 minutes, stirring well to combine all ingredients.
5. Assemble Lettuce Wraps: Spoon the turkey and vegetable filling into individual lettuce leaves, using them as wraps or cups to hold the filling.

6. Garnish and Serve: Garnish the turkey and vegetable lettuce wraps with sliced green onions, chopped fresh cilantro, and sesame seeds, if desired.
7. Enjoy: Serve the lettuce wraps immediately as a light and healthy meal or appetizer.

These turkey and vegetable lettuce wraps are packed with protein and nutrients, making them a great option for a quick and satisfying meal. The combination of savory turkey, colorful vegetables, and Asian-inspired flavors creates a delicious and balanced dish. Feel free to customize the filling with your favorite vegetables or spices. These lettuce wraps are also gluten-free and low-carb, perfect for those looking for a lighter meal option. Enjoy this flavorful and gut-friendly dish!

Cauliflower Rice Stir-Fry

Ingredients:

For the Cauliflower Rice:

- 1 large head of cauliflower
- 2 tablespoons olive oil or coconut oil
- Salt and pepper, to taste

For the Stir-Fry:

- 1 tablespoon sesame oil
- 2 cloves garlic, minced
- 1-inch piece of ginger, grated
- 1 small onion, finely chopped
- 1 bell pepper, diced
- 1 carrot, diced
- 1 cup frozen peas
- 2 tablespoons soy sauce or tamari (gluten-free option)
- 1 tablespoon rice vinegar
- 2 green onions, chopped (for garnish)
- Sesame seeds, for garnish

Optional Protein Additions:

- Cooked chicken, shrimp, tofu, or edamame

Instructions:

1. Prepare Cauliflower Rice: Cut the cauliflower into florets and discard the tough stem. Place the cauliflower florets in a food processor and pulse until it resembles rice or couscous texture.
2. Cook Cauliflower Rice: Heat 1 tablespoon of olive oil or coconut oil in a large skillet or wok over medium heat. Add the cauliflower rice and season with salt and pepper. Cook for 5-6 minutes, stirring occasionally, until the cauliflower is tender and slightly golden. Remove from the skillet and set aside.
3. Make Stir-Fry: In the same skillet or wok, heat the sesame oil over medium-high heat. Add minced garlic and grated ginger, and sauté for 1 minute until fragrant.

4. Add Vegetables: Add chopped onion, diced bell pepper, and diced carrot to the skillet. Stir-fry for 3-4 minutes until the vegetables start to soften.
5. Stir in Peas: Add frozen peas to the skillet and cook for another 2-3 minutes until heated through.
6. Combine Cauliflower Rice: Return the cooked cauliflower rice to the skillet with the vegetables. Mix everything together.
7. Add Sauce: In a small bowl, whisk together soy sauce or tamari and rice vinegar. Pour the sauce over the cauliflower rice and vegetables. Stir well to coat everything evenly.
8. Optional Protein: If desired, add cooked chicken, shrimp, tofu, or edamame to the cauliflower rice stir-fry. Stir to combine and heat through.
9. Garnish and Serve: Remove the skillet from heat. Garnish with chopped green onions and sesame seeds.
10. Enjoy: Serve the cauliflower rice stir-fry hot as a delicious and nutritious meal. It's a satisfying low-carb alternative to traditional rice-based stir-fries.

This cauliflower rice stir-fry is versatile and customizable. Feel free to add your favorite vegetables, protein sources, or spices to suit your taste preferences. It's a great option for those looking for a gut-friendly, gluten-free, and low-carb meal that's packed with nutrients. Enjoy this flavorful and healthy cauliflower rice stir-fry!

Spiced Lentil Soup

Ingredients:

- 1 tablespoon olive oil or coconut oil
- 1 onion, diced
- 2 carrots, diced
- 2 celery stalks, diced
- 3 cloves garlic, minced
- 1 tablespoon fresh ginger, grated
- 1 teaspoon ground cumin
- 1 teaspoon ground coriander
- 1/2 teaspoon turmeric
- 1/2 teaspoon paprika
- 1/4 teaspoon cayenne pepper (adjust to taste)
- 1 cup dried lentils (brown or green), rinsed
- 4 cups vegetable broth or water
- 1 (14 oz) can diced tomatoes
- 1 bay leaf
- Salt and pepper, to taste
- Juice of 1 lemon
- Fresh cilantro or parsley, chopped (for garnish)
- Plain yogurt or coconut yogurt (optional, for serving)

Instructions:

1. Sauté Aromatics: Heat the olive oil or coconut oil in a large pot or Dutch oven over medium heat. Add the diced onion, carrots, and celery. Sauté for 5-7 minutes until the vegetables start to soften.
2. Add Spices and Aromatics: Stir in the minced garlic, grated ginger, ground cumin, ground coriander, turmeric, paprika, and cayenne pepper. Cook for 1-2 minutes until fragrant.
3. Add Lentils and Liquid: Add the rinsed lentils, vegetable broth or water, diced tomatoes (with juices), and bay leaf to the pot. Stir to combine.
4. Simmer Soup: Bring the soup to a boil, then reduce the heat to low. Cover and simmer for about 20-25 minutes, or until the lentils are tender and cooked through.
5. Season and Finish: Season the soup with salt and pepper, adjusting to taste. Stir in the lemon juice for brightness.

6. Serve: Ladle the spiced lentil soup into bowls. Garnish with chopped fresh cilantro or parsley.
7. Optional: Serve with Yogurt: Serve the spiced lentil soup hot, optionally topped with a dollop of plain yogurt or coconut yogurt for creaminess.
8. Enjoy: Enjoy this flavorful and nutritious spiced lentil soup as a satisfying meal. It pairs well with crusty bread or a side salad.

This spiced lentil soup is not only delicious but also packed with plant-based protein, fiber, and essential nutrients. The aromatic spices add depth of flavor while the lentils provide a hearty texture. It's a perfect dish for chilly days and can be easily customized by adding additional vegetables or adjusting the level of spiciness according to your taste preferences. Enjoy this comforting and gut-friendly soup!

Baked Sweet Potatoes with Chickpea Curry

Ingredients:

For the Baked Sweet Potatoes:

- 4 medium sweet potatoes
- 1 tablespoon olive oil
- Salt and pepper, to taste

For the Chickpea Curry:

- 1 tablespoon coconut oil or olive oil
- 1 onion, finely chopped
- 3 cloves garlic, minced
- 1 tablespoon grated ginger
- 1 bell pepper, diced
- 1 zucchini, diced
- 1 can (15 oz) chickpeas (garbanzo beans), drained and rinsed
- 1 can (14 oz) diced tomatoes
- 1 can (14 oz) coconut milk
- 2 teaspoons curry powder
- 1 teaspoon ground cumin
- 1 teaspoon ground coriander
- 1/2 teaspoon turmeric
- Salt and pepper, to taste
- Fresh cilantro, chopped (for garnish)
- Cooked rice or quinoa, for serving (optional)

Instructions:

1. Prepare Baked Sweet Potatoes:
    - Preheat your oven to 400°F (200°C).
    - Scrub the sweet potatoes clean and pat them dry with a paper towel.
    - Prick the sweet potatoes several times with a fork.
    - Rub the sweet potatoes with olive oil and season with salt and pepper.
    - Place the sweet potatoes on a baking sheet lined with parchment paper.
    - Bake for 45-60 minutes, or until the sweet potatoes are tender and can be easily pierced with a fork.

2. Prepare Chickpea Curry:
   - In a large skillet or pot, heat coconut oil or olive oil over medium heat.
   - Add the chopped onion, minced garlic, and grated ginger. Sauté for 2-3 minutes until the onion becomes translucent.
   - Add the diced bell pepper and zucchini to the skillet. Cook for another 3-4 minutes until the vegetables start to soften.
   - Stir in the drained and rinsed chickpeas, diced tomatoes (with juices), and coconut milk.
   - Add curry powder, ground cumin, ground coriander, turmeric, salt, and pepper. Stir well to combine.
   - Bring the mixture to a simmer, then reduce the heat to low. Let it simmer for 15-20 minutes, stirring occasionally, until the curry thickens slightly and the flavors meld together.
3. Assemble and Serve:
   - To serve, split open each baked sweet potato and lightly mash the flesh with a fork.
   - Spoon the warm chickpea curry over the baked sweet potatoes.
   - Garnish with chopped fresh cilantro.
   - Serve the baked sweet potatoes with chickpea curry as a satisfying and flavorful meal.
   - Optionally, serve with cooked rice or quinoa on the side for a complete and filling dish.

This baked sweet potatoes with chickpea curry recipe is rich in flavor, packed with nutrients, and perfect for a comforting dinner. The combination of creamy sweet potatoes with spicy and aromatic chickpea curry creates a delightful harmony of textures and tastes. Enjoy this wholesome and gut-friendly meal!

Greek Yogurt Chicken Skewers

Ingredients:

- 1.5 lbs (680g) boneless, skinless chicken breasts, cut into cubes
- 1 cup plain Greek yogurt
- Juice of 1 lemon
- 3 cloves garlic, minced
- 1 tablespoon olive oil
- 1 tablespoon chopped fresh oregano (or 1 teaspoon dried oregano)
- 1 teaspoon ground cumin
- 1/2 teaspoon paprika
- Salt and pepper, to taste
- Wooden skewers, soaked in water for at least 30 minutes

Instructions:

1. Marinate the Chicken:
    - In a mixing bowl, combine the Greek yogurt, lemon juice, minced garlic, olive oil, chopped oregano, ground cumin, paprika, salt, and pepper. Mix well to combine into a smooth marinade.
    - Add the chicken cubes to the marinade, ensuring they are well coated. Cover the bowl with plastic wrap or transfer to a resealable plastic bag. Refrigerate and marinate for at least 1 hour, or preferably overnight for maximum flavor.
2. Preheat the Grill (or Oven):
    - Preheat your grill to medium-high heat. Alternatively, preheat your oven to 400°F (200°C) and line a baking sheet with parchment paper.
3. Assemble the Skewers:
    - Thread the marinated chicken cubes onto the soaked wooden skewers, leaving a little space between each piece.
4. Grill (or Bake) the Skewers:
    - If grilling: Place the chicken skewers on the preheated grill. Cook for about 8-10 minutes, turning occasionally, until the chicken is cooked through and slightly charred on the edges.
    - If baking: Arrange the chicken skewers on the prepared baking sheet. Bake in the preheated oven for 15-20 minutes, or until the chicken is fully cooked and lightly browned.
5. Serve the Chicken Skewers:
    - Once cooked, remove the chicken skewers from the grill or oven.

- Serve the Greek yogurt chicken skewers hot, garnished with fresh lemon wedges and additional chopped oregano if desired.

6. Optional Sides:
   - Enjoy the chicken skewers with a side of Greek salad, couscous, quinoa, or roasted vegetables for a complete meal.

These Greek yogurt chicken skewers are tender, juicy, and bursting with Mediterranean flavors. The Greek yogurt marinade keeps the chicken moist and adds a delightful tanginess to the dish. It's a perfect option for a healthy and satisfying meal that's suitable for any occasion. Enjoy these flavorful chicken skewers as a delicious and gut-friendly dish!

Eggplant Rollatini

Ingredients:

For the Eggplant:

- 2 medium eggplants, sliced lengthwise into 1/4-inch thick slices
- Salt, for drawing out moisture
- Olive oil, for brushing

For the Ricotta Filling:

- 1 1/2 cups ricotta cheese
- 1/2 cup grated Parmesan cheese
- 1 egg
- 2 tablespoons chopped fresh basil
- 1 clove garlic, minced
- Salt and pepper, to taste

For Assembling:

- 2 cups marinara sauce
- 1 cup shredded mozzarella cheese
- Fresh basil leaves, for garnish (optional)

Instructions:

1. Prepare the Eggplant:
    - Lay the eggplant slices on a baking sheet and sprinkle both sides generously with salt. Let them sit for about 30 minutes to draw out excess moisture.
    - After 30 minutes, rinse the eggplant slices under cold water and pat them dry with paper towels.
    - Preheat the oven to 400°F (200°C). Brush both sides of the eggplant slices with olive oil and place them on a baking sheet lined with parchment paper. Bake for about 15-20 minutes, flipping halfway through, until tender and lightly golden. Remove from the oven and let cool slightly.
2. Make the Ricotta Filling:

- In a bowl, combine the ricotta cheese, grated Parmesan cheese, egg, chopped fresh basil, minced garlic, salt, and pepper. Mix well to combine.

3. Assemble the Rollatini:
    - Spread a spoonful of marinara sauce on the bottom of a baking dish.
    - Take each eggplant slice and place a spoonful of the ricotta filling at one end. Roll up the eggplant slice and place it seam-side down in the baking dish.
    - Repeat with the remaining eggplant slices and ricotta filling.

4. Top with Marinara Sauce and Cheese:
    - Pour the remaining marinara sauce over the eggplant rollatini, covering them evenly.
    - Sprinkle shredded mozzarella cheese over the top.

5. Bake the Rollatini:
    - Cover the baking dish with foil and bake in the preheated oven for about 20-25 minutes.
    - Remove the foil and continue baking for an additional 10 minutes, or until the cheese is melted and bubbly.

6. Serve:
    - Garnish with fresh basil leaves, if desired, and serve the eggplant rollatini hot.

Eggplant Rollatini is a comforting and satisfying dish that's perfect for a special dinner or gathering. The creamy ricotta filling complements the tender eggplant beautifully, and the marinara sauce and melted mozzarella cheese add wonderful flavors. Enjoy this delicious Eggplant Rollatini as a main dish with a side salad or crusty bread. It's sure to be a hit with family and friends!

Spinach and Feta Stuffed Chicken Breast

Ingredients:

For the Stuffed Chicken:

- 4 boneless, skinless chicken breasts
- Salt and pepper, to taste
- 2 cups fresh spinach leaves, chopped
- 1/2 cup crumbled feta cheese
- 2 cloves garlic, minced
- 1 tablespoon olive oil
- 1 tablespoon dried Italian herbs (or use a mixture of oregano, basil, and thyme)
- Toothpicks or kitchen twine, for securing

For the Sauce (Optional):

- 1 tablespoon olive oil
- 2 cloves garlic, minced
- 1 can (14 oz) diced tomatoes
- 1 teaspoon dried Italian herbs
- Salt and pepper, to taste

Instructions:

1. Preheat the Oven:
    - Preheat your oven to 375°F (190°C).
2. Prepare the Chicken Breasts:
    - Use a sharp knife to carefully slice each chicken breast horizontally to create a pocket, taking care not to cut all the way through. Season the inside and outside of the chicken breasts with salt and pepper.
3. Make the Spinach and Feta Filling:
    - In a skillet, heat olive oil over medium heat. Add minced garlic and chopped spinach. Cook for 2-3 minutes until the spinach wilts. Remove from heat.
    - Stir in crumbled feta cheese and dried Italian herbs. Mix well to combine.
4. Stuff the Chicken Breasts:

- Spoon the spinach and feta mixture into the pockets of the chicken breasts, dividing it evenly among them. Use toothpicks or kitchen twine to secure the openings and hold the stuffing in place.

5. Sear the Chicken (Optional):
    - In an oven-safe skillet, heat a bit of olive oil over medium-high heat. Sear the stuffed chicken breasts for 2-3 minutes on each side until golden brown. This step adds flavor and helps seal in the juices.
6. Bake the Chicken:
    - If using an oven-safe skillet, transfer the skillet to the preheated oven. Alternatively, transfer the chicken breasts to a baking dish.
    - Bake for 20-25 minutes or until the chicken is cooked through and reaches an internal temperature of 165°F (74°C).
7. Make the Optional Sauce:
    - While the chicken is baking, prepare the sauce if desired. In a skillet, heat olive oil over medium heat. Add minced garlic and cook for 1 minute until fragrant.
    - Stir in diced tomatoes and dried Italian herbs. Season with salt and pepper. Simmer for 5-7 minutes until the sauce thickens slightly.
8. Serve:
    - Remove the toothpicks or kitchen twine from the stuffed chicken breasts.
    - Serve the spinach and feta stuffed chicken breasts hot, optionally topped with the tomato sauce.

Spinach and feta stuffed chicken breast is a delicious and impressive dish that's perfect for a special dinner. The combination of tender chicken, savory spinach, and creamy feta cheese creates a delightful flavor profile. Serve this dish with a side of roasted vegetables, rice, or salad for a complete and satisfying meal. Enjoy!

Shrimp and Avocado SaladQuinoa Stuffed Bell Peppers

Ingredients:

- 4 bell peppers, any color
- 1 cup quinoa, rinsed
- 2 cups vegetable broth or water
- 1 tablespoon olive oil
- 1 onion, chopped
- 2 cloves garlic, minced
- 1 zucchini, diced
- 1 cup corn kernels (fresh or frozen)
- 1 (15 oz) can black beans, drained and rinsed
- 1 teaspoon ground cumin
- 1 teaspoon chili powder
- Salt and pepper, to taste
- 1 cup shredded cheese (cheddar or Monterey Jack), optional

Instructions:

1. Prepare Bell Peppers: Preheat the oven to 375°F (190°C). Cut the tops off the bell peppers and remove the seeds and membranes. Place the bell peppers in a baking dish.
2. Cook Quinoa: In a saucepan, combine the quinoa and vegetable broth (or water). Bring to a boil, then reduce the heat to low, cover, and simmer for 15-20 minutes until the quinoa is cooked and fluffy.
3. Make Filling: In a large skillet, heat olive oil over medium heat. Add chopped onion and garlic, and sauté for 2-3 minutes until softened.
4. Add Vegetables and Beans: Stir in diced zucchini, corn kernels, black beans, ground cumin, chili powder, salt, and pepper. Cook for 5-6 minutes until the vegetables are tender.
5. Combine Quinoa and Filling: Add the cooked quinoa to the skillet with the vegetable mixture. Stir well to combine. Adjust seasoning if needed.
6. Stuff Bell Peppers: Spoon the quinoa and vegetable mixture into the hollowed-out bell peppers, pressing gently to pack the filling.
7. Bake: Cover the baking dish with foil and bake in the preheated oven for 25-30 minutes, or until the bell peppers are tender.
8. Optional Cheese Topping: If using cheese, remove the foil and sprinkle shredded cheese over the stuffed bell peppers. Return to the oven and bake for an additional 5 minutes until the cheese is melted and bubbly.

9. Serve: Remove the stuffed bell peppers from the oven and let cool slightly before serving. Enjoy these delicious and nutritious quinoa stuffed bell peppers!

These recipes for Shrimp and Avocado Salad and Quinoa Stuffed Bell Peppers are both flavorful, healthy, and perfect for a satisfying meal. Enjoy these dishes as part of your meal planning!

Roasted Brussels Sprouts with Balsamic Glaze

Ingredients:

- 1 pound Brussels sprouts, trimmed and halved
- 2 tablespoons olive oil
- Salt and pepper, to taste
- 2 tablespoons balsamic vinegar
- 1 tablespoon honey or maple syrup (optional, for sweetness)
- Optional toppings: grated Parmesan cheese, chopped pecans or walnuts

Instructions:

1. Preheat Oven:
    - Preheat your oven to 400°F (200°C).
2. Prepare Brussels Sprouts:
    - Trim the ends of the Brussels sprouts and cut them in half lengthwise.
    - Place the halved Brussels sprouts on a baking sheet lined with parchment paper.
3. Season and Roast:
    - Drizzle olive oil over the Brussels sprouts and toss to coat evenly. Season with salt and pepper to taste.
    - Spread the Brussels sprouts out in a single layer on the baking sheet.
4. Roast Brussels Sprouts:
    - Roast the Brussels sprouts in the preheated oven for 20-25 minutes, or until they are tender and golden brown, stirring halfway through for even cooking.
5. Make Balsamic Glaze:
    - While the Brussels sprouts are roasting, prepare the balsamic glaze. In a small saucepan, combine the balsamic vinegar and honey or maple syrup (if using).
    - Bring the mixture to a simmer over medium heat. Cook for 5-7 minutes, stirring occasionally, until the glaze thickens and reduces by about half. Remove from heat.
6. Finish and Serve:
    - Once the Brussels sprouts are roasted to perfection, transfer them to a serving dish.
    - Drizzle the balsamic glaze over the roasted Brussels sprouts.
    - Optional: Sprinkle grated Parmesan cheese and chopped nuts (such as pecans or walnuts) over the top for added flavor and texture.

- Serve immediately as a delicious side dish with your favorite main course.

Tips for Serving:

- This roasted Brussels sprouts dish pairs well with roasted chicken, grilled steak, or baked salmon.
- Customize the dish by adding crispy bacon bits or dried cranberries for a sweet and savory contrast.
- Adjust the sweetness of the balsamic glaze to your liking by adding more or less honey or maple syrup.
- Enjoy these flavorful roasted Brussels sprouts with balsamic glaze as a healthy and satisfying addition to your meal!

This recipe is simple yet impressive, making it a great choice for weeknight dinners or special occasions. Roasting Brussels sprouts brings out their natural sweetness and caramelizes their edges, while the tangy balsamic glaze adds a delightful flavor boost. Give this recipe a try and enjoy the deliciousness of roasted Brussels sprouts with balsamic glaze!

Thai Coconut Chicken Soup

Ingredients:

- 1 tablespoon vegetable oil
- 1 small onion, thinly sliced
- 2 cloves garlic, minced
- 1-inch piece of ginger, peeled and grated
- 2 lemongrass stalks, bruised and chopped into 2-inch pieces
- 3-4 kaffir lime leaves (optional)
- 2-3 Thai red chilies, thinly sliced (adjust to taste)
- 1 pound (450g) boneless, skinless chicken breasts or thighs, thinly sliced
- 4 cups chicken broth
- 1 can (14 oz) coconut milk
- 1 tablespoon fish sauce (or soy sauce for vegetarian/vegan option)
- 1 tablespoon lime juice
- 1 tablespoon brown sugar (optional, to balance flavors)
- Salt, to taste
- Fresh cilantro leaves, for garnish
- Sliced red chilies, for garnish (optional)

Instructions:

1. Prepare Aromatics:
   - In a large pot or Dutch oven, heat the vegetable oil over medium heat. Add the sliced onion, minced garlic, grated ginger, lemongrass pieces, kaffir lime leaves (if using), and sliced Thai red chilies. Sauté for 2-3 minutes until fragrant.
2. Add Chicken:
   - Add the thinly sliced chicken to the pot. Cook for 4-5 minutes until the chicken starts to turn opaque.
3. Simmer Soup:
   - Pour in the chicken broth and bring the soup to a gentle simmer. Let it simmer for about 10 minutes until the chicken is cooked through.
4. Add Coconut Milk and Seasonings:
   - Stir in the coconut milk, fish sauce (or soy sauce), lime juice, and brown sugar (if using). Taste and adjust the seasoning with salt as needed.
5. Simmer Further:
   - Allow the soup to simmer for another 5 minutes to allow the flavors to meld together.

6. Remove Aromatics:
    - Use tongs to remove the lemongrass stalks, kaffir lime leaves, and any large pieces of ginger or garlic from the soup.
7. Serve:
    - Ladle the Thai coconut chicken soup into bowls. Garnish with fresh cilantro leaves and sliced red chilies for a pop of color and extra spice.
8. Enjoy:
    - Serve the Thai coconut chicken soup hot as a comforting and flavorful meal.

Tips for Serving:

- Serve the soup over steamed jasmine rice or rice noodles for a more substantial meal.
- Customize the spice level by adjusting the amount of Thai red chilies used.
- For added texture and flavor, you can add sliced mushrooms, cherry tomatoes, or baby corn to the soup.
- This Thai coconut chicken soup pairs well with fresh lime wedges and Thai basil leaves.

Enjoy this aromatic and creamy Thai Coconut Chicken Soup as a warming and satisfying dish that's perfect for any occasion. It's a delightful blend of sweet, savory, and spicy flavors that will transport you to Thailand with every spoonful!

Lemon Garlic Shrimp

Ingredients:

- 1 pound (450g) large shrimp, peeled and deveined
- 4 tablespoons unsalted butter
- 4 cloves garlic, minced
- Zest of 1 lemon
- Juice of 1 lemon
- Salt and pepper, to taste
- Red pepper flakes, to taste (optional)
- Chopped fresh parsley, for garnish

Instructions:

1. Prepare Shrimp:
    - Pat the shrimp dry with paper towels and season with salt and pepper.
2. Cook Shrimp:
    - In a large skillet or frying pan, melt 2 tablespoons of butter over medium-high heat.
    - Add the shrimp to the skillet in a single layer and cook for 1-2 minutes per side until they turn pink and opaque. Remove the cooked shrimp from the skillet and set aside.
3. Make Lemon Garlic Butter Sauce:
    - In the same skillet, melt the remaining 2 tablespoons of butter over medium heat.
    - Add minced garlic and cook for about 1 minute until fragrant.
4. Combine Lemon and Zest:
    - Add the lemon zest and lemon juice to the skillet. Stir well to combine with the garlic butter sauce.
5. Add Shrimp Back to the Skillet:
    - Return the cooked shrimp to the skillet and toss to coat them evenly with the lemon garlic butter sauce.
    - Cook for another minute to warm up the shrimp.
6. Season and Garnish:
    - Season with additional salt and pepper to taste. Add red pepper flakes for a bit of heat, if desired.
    - Garnish with chopped fresh parsley for color and freshness.
7. Serve:
    - Serve the lemon garlic shrimp immediately while hot.

- Enjoy as an appetizer, main dish, or serve over pasta, rice, or a fresh salad.

Tips for Serving:

- Serve the lemon garlic shrimp with crusty bread to soak up the delicious sauce.
- This dish pairs well with steamed vegetables, such as asparagus or green beans.
- Customize the flavor by adding other herbs like chopped basil or thyme.
- For a complete meal, serve the lemon garlic shrimp over cooked pasta or alongside a side of rice.

This Lemon Garlic Shrimp recipe is perfect for a quick and satisfying meal that's full of bright and zesty flavors. It's a versatile dish that can be enjoyed on its own or paired with your favorite sides. Give it a try for a delicious seafood dinner!

Baked Cod with Tomato and Olive Relish

Ingredients:

For the Baked Cod:

- 4 cod fillets (about 6 ounces each), skinless and boneless
- Salt and pepper, to taste
- 2 tablespoons olive oil
- 2 cloves garlic, minced
- 1 lemon, sliced (for garnish)

For the Tomato and Olive Relish:

- 1 cup cherry tomatoes, halved
- 1/2 cup pitted Kalamata olives, chopped
- 2 tablespoons capers, drained
- 2 tablespoons chopped fresh parsley
- 1 tablespoon chopped fresh basil
- 1 tablespoon chopped fresh oregano (or 1 teaspoon dried oregano)
- 2 tablespoons olive oil
- 1 tablespoon red wine vinegar
- Salt and pepper, to taste

Instructions:

1. Preheat the Oven:
   - Preheat your oven to 400°F (200°C).
2. Prepare the Cod Fillets:
   - Pat the cod fillets dry with paper towels and season both sides with salt and pepper.
3. Bake the Cod:
   - Place the cod fillets in a baking dish. Drizzle olive oil over the fillets and sprinkle minced garlic on top.
   - Bake in the preheated oven for 12-15 minutes, or until the cod is opaque and flakes easily with a fork.
4. Make the Tomato and Olive Relish:
   - In a medium bowl, combine the halved cherry tomatoes, chopped Kalamata olives, capers, chopped parsley, basil, and oregano.

- Drizzle olive oil and red wine vinegar over the tomato and olive mixture. Season with salt and pepper to taste. Toss to combine.
5. Serve the Baked Cod:
    - Remove the baked cod fillets from the oven.
    - Spoon the tomato and olive relish over the baked cod fillets.
6. Garnish and Serve:
    - Garnish the dish with fresh lemon slices.
    - Serve the baked cod with tomato and olive relish immediately, alongside steamed vegetables, rice, or crusty bread.

Tips for Serving:

- Feel free to customize the relish by adding other ingredients such as diced red onion, chopped bell peppers, or a pinch of crushed red pepper flakes for heat.
- This dish pairs well with a side of couscous, quinoa, or roasted potatoes.
- For a complete meal, serve the baked cod with a fresh green salad dressed with lemon vinaigrette.

Enjoy this baked cod with tomato and olive relish as a delicious and satisfying seafood dish that's perfect for any occasion. The combination of tender cod and flavorful Mediterranean-inspired relish creates a wonderful balance of flavors and textures. Bon appétit!

Butternut Squash and Kale Salad

Ingredients:

For the Salad:

- 1 small butternut squash, peeled, seeded, and diced into cubes
- 1 tablespoon olive oil
- Salt and pepper, to taste
- 1 bunch kale (about 6-8 cups), stems removed and leaves torn into bite-sized pieces
- 1/4 cup dried cranberries or cherries
- 1/4 cup toasted pumpkin seeds or pecans

For the Dressing:

- 3 tablespoons extra-virgin olive oil
- 2 tablespoons apple cider vinegar or balsamic vinegar
- 1 tablespoon maple syrup or honey
- 1 teaspoon Dijon mustard
- Salt and pepper, to taste

Instructions:

1. Roast the Butternut Squash:
    - Preheat your oven to 400°F (200°C).
    - Place the diced butternut squash on a baking sheet. Drizzle with olive oil, season with salt and pepper, and toss to coat evenly.
    - Roast in the preheated oven for 20-25 minutes, or until the squash is tender and lightly caramelized. Allow it to cool slightly.
2. Prepare the Kale:
    - In a large mixing bowl, add the torn kale leaves.
    - Massage the kale with clean hands for a few minutes until it becomes tender and slightly wilted.
3. Assemble the Salad:
    - Add the roasted butternut squash, dried cranberries or cherries, and toasted pumpkin seeds or pecans to the bowl with the kale.
4. Make the Dressing:

- In a small bowl or jar, whisk together the extra-virgin olive oil, apple cider vinegar or balsamic vinegar, maple syrup or honey, Dijon mustard, salt, and pepper until well combined.
5. Dress the Salad:
    - Pour the dressing over the salad ingredients.
    - Toss everything together until the salad is well coated with the dressing.
6. Serve:
    - Transfer the butternut squash and kale salad to a serving dish or individual plates.
    - Enjoy immediately as a nutritious and flavorful side dish or light meal.

Tips for Serving:

- Feel free to customize this salad by adding other ingredients such as sliced apples or pears, crumbled feta or goat cheese, or cooked quinoa or farro for added texture and protein.
- You can substitute other winter squash varieties like acorn squash or kabocha squash for the butternut squash.
- For extra flavor, sprinkle some freshly grated Parmesan cheese or a pinch of cinnamon over the roasted butternut squash before adding it to the salad.
- This salad can be enjoyed warm or at room temperature.

This Butternut Squash and Kale Salad is not only delicious but also packed with nutrients and colors. It's perfect for autumn and winter seasons when butternut squash is in season. Enjoy this wholesome salad as a healthy addition to your meal rotation!

Turkey Meatballs in Tomato Sauce

Ingredients:

For the Turkey Meatballs:

- 1 pound ground turkey (preferably lean)
- 1/2 cup breadcrumbs (or almond flour for a gluten-free option)
- 1/4 cup grated Parmesan cheese
- 1 egg, lightly beaten
- 2 cloves garlic, minced
- 1 tablespoon fresh parsley, finely chopped
- 1 teaspoon dried oregano
- 1/2 teaspoon salt
- 1/4 teaspoon black pepper

For the Tomato Sauce:

- 1 tablespoon olive oil
- 1 small onion, finely chopped
- 2 cloves garlic, minced
- 1 can (14 oz) crushed tomatoes
- 1 can (14 oz) diced tomatoes
- 1 teaspoon dried basil
- 1 teaspoon dried oregano
- Salt and pepper, to taste
- Optional: Red pepper flakes, to taste (for heat)
- Fresh basil or parsley, chopped (for garnish)

Instructions:

1. Preheat the Oven:
    - Preheat your oven to 400°F (200°C). Line a baking sheet with parchment paper or lightly grease it with olive oil.
2. Make the Turkey Meatballs:
    - In a large mixing bowl, combine the ground turkey, breadcrumbs, grated Parmesan cheese, beaten egg, minced garlic, chopped parsley, dried oregano, salt, and pepper.
    - Mix the ingredients together until well combined.

- Shape the mixture into meatballs, about 1 to 1.5 inches in diameter, and place them on the prepared baking sheet.
- Bake the meatballs in the preheated oven for 15-20 minutes, or until cooked through and lightly browned.

3. Prepare the Tomato Sauce:
    - While the meatballs are baking, heat olive oil in a large skillet over medium heat.
    - Add the finely chopped onion and sauté for 3-4 minutes until softened.
    - Stir in the minced garlic and cook for an additional 1 minute until fragrant.
4. Simmer the Sauce:
    - Add the crushed tomatoes, diced tomatoes (with their juices), dried basil, and dried oregano to the skillet.
    - Season with salt, pepper, and red pepper flakes (if using).
    - Bring the sauce to a simmer, then reduce the heat to low and let it simmer gently for about 10 minutes to allow the flavors to meld together.
5. Combine Meatballs and Sauce:
    - Once the meatballs are cooked, transfer them to the skillet with the tomato sauce.
    - Gently stir to coat the meatballs with the sauce.
    - Allow the meatballs to simmer in the sauce for an additional 5-10 minutes.
6. Serve:
    - Serve the turkey meatballs in tomato sauce hot, garnished with chopped fresh basil or parsley.
    - Enjoy as a main dish with pasta, rice, or crusty bread, or serve them over zucchini noodles for a low-carb option.

Tips for Serving:

- Feel free to add additional vegetables to the sauce, such as diced bell peppers, mushrooms, or spinach, to boost the nutritional content.
- These turkey meatballs in tomato sauce also make delicious meatball subs or can be served as appetizers for parties.
- Store any leftovers in an airtight container in the refrigerator for up to 3-4 days or freeze for longer storage.

This recipe for turkey meatballs in tomato sauce is a comforting and satisfying dish that the whole family will love. It's perfect for weeknight dinners and can be easily customized to suit your taste preferences. Enjoy!

Roasted Cauliflower Tacos

Ingredients:

For the Roasted Cauliflower:

- 1 medium head of cauliflower, cut into florets
- 2 tablespoons olive oil
- 1 teaspoon chili powder
- 1/2 teaspoon ground cumin
- 1/2 teaspoon smoked paprika
- 1/4 teaspoon garlic powder
- Salt and pepper, to taste

For Serving:

- 8 small tortillas (corn or flour)
- Shredded cabbage or lettuce
- Sliced avocado or guacamole
- Sliced radishes
- Chopped fresh cilantro
- Lime wedges
- Hot sauce or salsa (optional)

Instructions:

1. Preheat the Oven:
   - Preheat your oven to 425°F (220°C). Line a baking sheet with parchment paper or lightly grease it with olive oil.
2. Prepare the Cauliflower:
   - In a large bowl, toss the cauliflower florets with olive oil, chili powder, cumin, smoked paprika, garlic powder, salt, and pepper until evenly coated.
3. Roast the Cauliflower:
   - Spread the seasoned cauliflower florets in a single layer on the prepared baking sheet.
   - Roast in the preheated oven for 20-25 minutes, or until the cauliflower is tender and caramelized, stirring halfway through cooking.
4. Assemble the Tacos:
   - Warm the tortillas in a dry skillet or microwave.
   - Fill each tortilla with a generous portion of roasted cauliflower.

5. Add Toppings:
   - Top the cauliflower with shredded cabbage or lettuce, sliced avocado or guacamole, sliced radishes, and chopped cilantro.
6. Serve:
   - Squeeze fresh lime juice over the tacos and drizzle with hot sauce or salsa, if desired.
   - Serve the roasted cauliflower tacos immediately and enjoy!

Tips for Serving:

- Customize the toppings based on your preferences. Other great toppings include diced tomatoes, pickled onions, crumbled cotija cheese, or a dollop of sour cream or Greek yogurt.
- Add protein by including black beans, refried beans, or grilled tofu alongside the roasted cauliflower.
- For extra flavor, drizzle a creamy cilantro lime dressing or chipotle mayo over the tacos.
- Serve with a side of Mexican rice, refried beans, or a fresh salad to complete the meal.

These roasted cauliflower tacos are perfect for a meatless dinner option that's packed with flavor and texture. They are also great for gatherings and can be easily customized to accommodate various dietary preferences. Enjoy these delicious and nutritious tacos any day of the week!

Lemon Rosemary Grilled Chicken

Ingredients:

- 4 boneless, skinless chicken breasts
- Zest and juice of 2 lemons
- 3-4 cloves garlic, minced
- 2 tablespoons fresh rosemary, finely chopped
- 1/4 cup olive oil
- Salt and pepper, to taste

Instructions:

1. Prepare the Marinade:
    - In a bowl, whisk together the lemon zest, lemon juice, minced garlic, chopped rosemary, olive oil, salt, and pepper.
2. Marinate the Chicken:
    - Place the chicken breasts in a shallow dish or resealable plastic bag.
    - Pour the marinade over the chicken, ensuring that all pieces are coated evenly.
    - Cover the dish or seal the bag and refrigerate for at least 1 hour, or ideally up to 4 hours, to allow the flavors to penetrate the chicken.
3. Preheat the Grill:
    - Preheat your grill to medium-high heat (about 400°F or 200°C).
4. Grill the Chicken:
    - Remove the chicken breasts from the marinade and discard the excess marinade.
    - Place the chicken on the preheated grill and cook for 6-7 minutes per side, or until the chicken is cooked through and reaches an internal temperature of 165°F (75°C).
5. Rest and Serve:
    - Once cooked, transfer the grilled chicken breasts to a plate or cutting board and let them rest for a few minutes.
    - Slice the chicken breasts and serve hot.
6. Garnish and Enjoy:
    - Garnish the lemon rosemary grilled chicken with additional fresh rosemary and lemon wedges, if desired.
    - Serve alongside your favorite side dishes such as grilled vegetables, rice, or a fresh salad.

Tips for Grilling:

- Make sure to preheat your grill properly before adding the chicken to ensure even cooking and beautiful grill marks.
- Use a meat thermometer to check the internal temperature of the chicken. The thickest part of the chicken breast should reach 165°F (75°C) for safe consumption.
- If using wooden skewers or bamboo sticks, soak them in water for about 30 minutes before grilling to prevent them from burning.

This lemon rosemary grilled chicken recipe is simple yet incredibly flavorful. The combination of citrusy lemon, aromatic rosemary, and garlic infuses the chicken with delicious Mediterranean-inspired flavors. Enjoy this grilled chicken as a main course for a summer barbecue or any time you crave a tasty and satisfying meal!

Chickpea and Spinach Curry

Ingredients:

- 2 tablespoons vegetable oil
- 1 onion, finely chopped
- 3 cloves garlic, minced
- 1-inch piece of ginger, grated
- 1 green chili, finely chopped (adjust to taste)
- 1 teaspoon cumin seeds
- 1 teaspoon ground coriander
- 1 teaspoon ground cumin
- 1/2 teaspoon turmeric powder
- 1/2 teaspoon paprika or chili powder (adjust to taste)
- 1 can (15 oz) chickpeas, drained and rinsed (or 1.5 cups cooked chickpeas)
- 1 can (14 oz) diced tomatoes
- 1 teaspoon sugar (optional, to balance acidity)
- Salt, to taste
- 1 cup chopped fresh spinach leaves
- 1/4 cup chopped fresh cilantro (coriander) leaves, for garnish
- Cooked rice or naan bread, for serving

Instructions:

1. Sauté Aromatics:
    - Heat the vegetable oil in a large skillet or saucepan over medium heat.
    - Add the chopped onion and sauté for 5-6 minutes until softened and translucent.
2. Add Spices:
    - Stir in the minced garlic, grated ginger, green chili, and cumin seeds. Sauté for another 1-2 minutes until fragrant.
3. Add Ground Spices:
    - Add the ground coriander, ground cumin, turmeric powder, and paprika or chili powder to the skillet. Stir well to coat the onions and spices.
4. Cook Chickpeas and Tomatoes:
    - Add the drained chickpeas and diced tomatoes (with their juices) to the skillet.
    - Stir in the sugar (if using) and season with salt to taste.

- Bring the mixture to a simmer and cook for 10-12 minutes, stirring occasionally, until the sauce thickens slightly and the flavors meld together.
5. Add Spinach:
    - Stir in the chopped spinach leaves and cook for an additional 2-3 minutes until the spinach wilts.
6. Adjust Seasoning and Serve:
    - Taste the chickpea and spinach curry and adjust the seasoning with salt and additional spices if desired.
    - Garnish with chopped fresh cilantro (coriander) leaves.
7. Serve:
    - Serve the chickpea and spinach curry hot with cooked rice or warm naan bread.

Tips for Serving:

- Customize the level of spice by adjusting the amount of green chili and paprika or chili powder.
- For added creaminess, stir in a few tablespoons of coconut milk or plain yogurt towards the end of cooking.
- This curry also pairs well with quinoa or couscous instead of rice.
- Leftovers can be stored in an airtight container in the refrigerator for up to 3-4 days. The flavors will continue to develop over time.

Enjoy this flavorful and satisfying chickpea and spinach curry as a hearty vegetarian meal that's perfect for weeknight dinners. It's wholesome, nutritious, and packed with protein from the chickpeas and vitamins from the spinach. Serve it with your favorite side for a complete and delicious meal!

Asian Cabbage Salad

Ingredients:

For the Salad:

- 1 small head of Napa cabbage, thinly sliced (about 4 cups)
- 1 cup red cabbage, thinly sliced
- 1 red bell pepper, thinly sliced
- 1 large carrot, julienned or grated
- 1/2 cucumber, thinly sliced
- 3 green onions, thinly sliced
- 1/4 cup chopped fresh cilantro or parsley
- 1/4 cup chopped roasted peanuts or cashews (optional, for garnish)
- Sesame seeds, for garnish

For the Sesame Ginger Dressing:

- 3 tablespoons soy sauce (use tamari for gluten-free)
- 2 tablespoons rice vinegar
- 1 tablespoon sesame oil
- 1 tablespoon honey or maple syrup
- 1 tablespoon grated fresh ginger
- 1 clove garlic, minced
- 1 tablespoon neutral-flavored oil (such as vegetable or grapeseed oil)
- 1 teaspoon sriracha or chili garlic sauce (optional, for heat)

Instructions:

1. Prepare the Vegetables:
    - In a large salad bowl, combine the sliced Napa cabbage, red cabbage, red bell pepper, julienned carrot, sliced cucumber, green onions, and chopped cilantro or parsley.
2. Make the Sesame Ginger Dressing:
    - In a small bowl or jar, whisk together the soy sauce, rice vinegar, sesame oil, honey or maple syrup, grated ginger, minced garlic, neutral-flavored oil, and sriracha or chili garlic sauce (if using).
3. Assemble the Salad:
    - Pour the sesame ginger dressing over the prepared vegetables in the salad bowl.

- Toss everything together until the vegetables are evenly coated with the dressing.
4. Garnish and Serve:
    - Garnish the Asian cabbage salad with chopped roasted peanuts or cashews (if using) and sesame seeds.
    - Serve the salad immediately as a side dish or light meal.

Tips for Serving:

- For added protein, you can top the salad with grilled chicken, shrimp, tofu, or edamame.
- Customize the salad by adding other vegetables such as snow peas, bean sprouts, or shredded daikon radish.
- Make the salad ahead of time by preparing the vegetables and dressing separately. Toss them together just before serving to keep the vegetables crisp.
- Adjust the sweetness and spiciness of the dressing to suit your taste preferences.

This Asian cabbage salad is vibrant, flavorful, and packed with nutrients. It's a great dish to enjoy during warmer months or alongside Asian-inspired main courses. The sesame ginger dressing adds a delicious umami flavor that complements the crunchy texture of the cabbage and vegetables. Give this salad a try for a delightful and healthy meal option!

Baked Falafel with Tahini Sauce

Ingredients:

For the Baked Falafel:

- 2 cans (15 oz each) chickpeas, drained and rinsed
- 1/2 cup chopped fresh parsley
- 1/2 cup chopped fresh cilantro
- 4 cloves garlic, minced
- 1 small onion, chopped
- 2 tablespoons olive oil
- 2 tablespoons lemon juice
- 2 teaspoons ground cumin
- 2 teaspoons ground coriander
- 1 teaspoon salt
- 1/2 teaspoon black pepper
- 1/2 teaspoon baking soda
- 1/4 cup chickpea flour or all-purpose flour (for binding)

For the Tahini Sauce:

- 1/2 cup tahini (sesame seed paste)
- 1/4 cup water
- 2 tablespoons lemon juice
- 1 clove garlic, minced
- Salt, to taste

For Serving:

- Pita bread or wraps
- Sliced cucumbers, tomatoes, and red onions
- Chopped fresh parsley or cilantro

Instructions:

1. Prepare the Baked Falafel:
    - Preheat your oven to 375°F (190°C) and line a baking sheet with parchment paper.

- In a food processor, combine the chickpeas, chopped parsley, chopped cilantro, minced garlic, chopped onion, olive oil, lemon juice, ground cumin, ground coriander, salt, black pepper, and baking soda.
- Pulse the mixture until it forms a coarse paste, but be careful not to over-process.
- Transfer the falafel mixture to a mixing bowl and stir in the chickpea flour or all-purpose flour until well combined.

2. Shape and Bake the Falafel:
    - Scoop about 2 tablespoons of the falafel mixture and shape it into a small patty using your hands.
    - Place the falafel patties on the prepared baking sheet.
    - Bake in the preheated oven for 25-30 minutes, flipping halfway through, until the falafel patties are golden brown and crispy.
3. Prepare the Tahini Sauce:
    - In a small bowl, whisk together the tahini, water, lemon juice, minced garlic, and salt until smooth and creamy. Add more water if needed to achieve desired consistency.
4. Serve the Baked Falafel:
    - Warm the pita bread or wraps.
    - Fill each pita or wrap with baked falafel patties, sliced cucumbers, tomatoes, and red onions.
    - Drizzle with tahini sauce and sprinkle with chopped fresh parsley or cilantro.
    - Serve the baked falafel with tahini sauce immediately and enjoy!

Tips for Serving:

- For extra crispiness, you can brush the falafel patties with a little olive oil before baking.
- Make-ahead tip: You can prepare the falafel mixture in advance and refrigerate it until ready to bake. Shape and bake the falafel just before serving.
- Serve the baked falafel as a sandwich, wrap, or salad topping. It's also delicious on its own as an appetizer.
- Customize the falafel toppings based on your preferences. Add pickled vegetables, hot sauce, or additional herbs for extra flavor.

This baked falafel with tahini sauce recipe is a fantastic option for a satisfying and wholesome meal. The falafel patties are crispy on the outside and tender on the inside, and the creamy tahini sauce complements them perfectly. Enjoy this delicious dish with your favorite Mediterranean-inspired sides!

Salmon Cakes with Dill Yogurt Sauce

Ingredients:

For the Salmon Cakes:

- 2 cans (14.75 oz each) salmon, drained and flaked (or equivalent cooked salmon)
- 1/2 cup breadcrumbs (panko or regular)
- 1/4 cup finely chopped green onions (scallions)
- 2 tablespoons chopped fresh dill
- 2 tablespoons chopped fresh parsley
- 1 tablespoon Dijon mustard
- 1 tablespoon lemon juice
- 1 teaspoon Worcestershire sauce
- 1/2 teaspoon garlic powder
- 1/2 teaspoon salt
- 1/4 teaspoon black pepper
- 2 large eggs, lightly beaten
- 2-3 tablespoons olive oil, for frying

For the Dill Yogurt Sauce:

- 1 cup plain Greek yogurt
- 2 tablespoons chopped fresh dill
- 1 tablespoon lemon juice
- Salt and pepper, to taste

Instructions:

1. Prepare the Dill Yogurt Sauce:
    - In a bowl, combine the Greek yogurt, chopped fresh dill, lemon juice, salt, and pepper. Mix well until smooth and creamy. Adjust seasoning to taste. Cover and refrigerate until ready to serve.
2. Make the Salmon Cakes:
    - In a large mixing bowl, combine the flaked salmon, breadcrumbs, chopped green onions, chopped dill, chopped parsley, Dijon mustard, lemon juice, Worcestershire sauce, garlic powder, salt, and black pepper.
    - Add the lightly beaten eggs to the mixture and stir until everything is well combined. The mixture should hold together when shaped into patties. If it's too wet, add more breadcrumbs.

3. Shape and Cook the Salmon Cakes:
   - Divide the salmon mixture into 8 equal portions.
   - Shape each portion into a patty, about 1/2-inch thick.
   - Heat olive oil in a large skillet over medium heat.
   - Add the salmon cakes to the skillet (in batches if needed) and cook for 3-4 minutes on each side, or until golden brown and cooked through. Use a spatula to carefully flip the cakes.
4. Serve:
   - Transfer the cooked salmon cakes to a serving platter.
   - Serve the salmon cakes hot with the dill yogurt sauce on the side.
   - Garnish with additional fresh dill or lemon wedges if desired.

Tips for Serving:

- These salmon cakes can be served as a main course with a side salad or roasted vegetables.
- They also make a great appetizer or party snack served with the dill yogurt sauce for dipping.
- Customize the salmon cakes by adding chopped bell peppers, celery, or capers for extra flavor and texture.
- Leftover salmon cakes can be refrigerated for a few days and reheated in the oven or microwave.

Enjoy these delicious salmon cakes with dill yogurt sauce for a tasty and satisfying meal that's easy to make at home!

Lentil and Sweet Potato Shepherd's Pie

Ingredients:

For the Lentil Filling:

- 1 cup dried green or brown lentils, rinsed
- 2 tablespoons olive oil
- 1 onion, chopped
- 2 carrots, diced
- 2 celery stalks, diced
- 2 cloves garlic, minced
- 1 teaspoon dried thyme
- 1 teaspoon dried rosemary
- 1 teaspoon paprika
- 1 can (14 oz) diced tomatoes
- 1 cup vegetable broth
- Salt and pepper, to taste
- 1 cup frozen peas (optional)
- Chopped fresh parsley, for garnish

For the Sweet Potato Topping:

- 2 large sweet potatoes, peeled and diced
- 2 tablespoons butter or olive oil
- 1/4 cup milk (dairy or plant-based)
- Salt and pepper, to taste

Instructions:

1. Prepare the Lentil Filling:
    - In a saucepan, combine the rinsed lentils with 2 cups of water. Bring to a boil, then reduce heat and simmer for about 15-20 minutes, or until the lentils are tender but still hold their shape. Drain any excess water and set aside.
2. Prepare the Sweet Potato Topping:
    - While the lentils are cooking, place the diced sweet potatoes in a separate pot and cover with water. Bring to a boil, then reduce heat and simmer for 15-20 minutes, or until the sweet potatoes are fork-tender.

- Drain the cooked sweet potatoes and return them to the pot.
- Add butter or olive oil, milk, salt, and pepper to the pot with the sweet potatoes. Mash until smooth and creamy. Adjust seasoning to taste.

3. Make the Lentil Filling:
   - In a large skillet or pan, heat olive oil over medium heat. Add chopped onion, carrots, and celery. Sauté for 5-7 minutes, or until the vegetables start to soften.
   - Add minced garlic, dried thyme, dried rosemary, and paprika. Cook for another 1-2 minutes until fragrant.
   - Stir in the cooked lentils, diced tomatoes (with their juices), and vegetable broth. Bring to a simmer and cook for 10-15 minutes, stirring occasionally, until the mixture thickens slightly.
   - Season with salt and pepper to taste. If using frozen peas, add them during the last few minutes of cooking.
4. Assemble and Bake:
   - Preheat your oven to 375°F (190°C).
   - Transfer the lentil filling to a baking dish or oven-safe skillet.
   - Spread the mashed sweet potatoes evenly over the lentil filling.
   - Use a fork to create a decorative pattern on the surface of the sweet potatoes.
5. Bake the Shepherd's Pie:
   - Place the baking dish in the preheated oven and bake for 20-25 minutes, or until the filling is bubbly and the sweet potato topping is lightly golden on the edges.
6. Serve:
   - Remove the shepherd's pie from the oven and let it cool slightly before serving.
   - Garnish with chopped fresh parsley and serve warm.

Tips for Serving:

- Feel free to customize the vegetables in the lentil filling based on what you have on hand or your preferences.
- You can add grated cheese on top of the sweet potato topping before baking for extra richness.
- Leftovers of this lentil and sweet potato shepherd's pie can be stored in the refrigerator for a few days and reheated in the oven or microwave.

Enjoy this delicious and nourishing lentil and sweet potato shepherd's pie as a satisfying meal for lunch or dinner. It's packed with protein, fiber, and wholesome flavors that will warm you up from the inside out!

Quinoa Tabouleh Salad

Ingredients:

For the Salad:

- 1 cup quinoa
- 2 cups water or vegetable broth
- 1 cucumber, finely diced
- 2 tomatoes, finely diced
- 1 bunch fresh parsley, finely chopped
- 1/2 bunch fresh mint leaves, finely chopped
- 3 green onions, finely chopped
- 1/4 cup finely chopped red onion (optional)
- Salt and pepper, to taste

For the Lemon Dressing:

- 1/4 cup extra-virgin olive oil
- 1/4 cup fresh lemon juice (about 1-2 lemons)
- 1 clove garlic, minced
- 1 teaspoon honey or maple syrup (optional, for sweetness)
- Salt and pepper, to taste

Optional Additions:

- 1/2 cup cooked chickpeas (garbanzo beans)
- 1/2 cup chopped cucumber
- 1/4 cup crumbled feta cheese
- 1/4 cup chopped Kalamata olives

Instructions:

1. Cook the Quinoa:
    - Rinse the quinoa under cold water using a fine-mesh sieve.
    - In a saucepan, combine the rinsed quinoa with water or vegetable broth.
    - Bring to a boil, then reduce heat to low, cover, and simmer for 15-20 minutes, or until the quinoa is cooked and the liquid is absorbed.

- Remove from heat and let it sit, covered, for 5 minutes. Fluff the quinoa with a fork and allow it to cool completely.
2. Prepare the Vegetables and Herbs:
    - While the quinoa is cooking, prepare the vegetables and herbs.
    - Finely dice the cucumber, tomatoes, and red onion (if using).
    - Chop the fresh parsley, mint leaves, and green onions.
3. Make the Lemon Dressing:
    - In a small bowl, whisk together the extra-virgin olive oil, fresh lemon juice, minced garlic, honey or maple syrup (if using), salt, and pepper. Adjust seasoning to taste.
4. Assemble the Salad:
    - In a large mixing bowl, combine the cooked and cooled quinoa with the diced cucumber, tomatoes, chopped parsley, mint, green onions, and red onion (if using).
    - Pour the lemon dressing over the salad and toss everything together until well combined.
    - Season with additional salt and pepper to taste.
5. Optional Additions:
    - For added protein and texture, mix in cooked chickpeas, chopped cucumber, crumbled feta cheese, or chopped Kalamata olives.
6. Chill and Serve:
    - Refrigerate the quinoa tabbouleh salad for at least 30 minutes to allow the flavors to meld together.
    - Serve chilled as a refreshing side dish or light meal.

Tips for Serving:

- This quinoa tabbouleh salad can be made ahead of time and stored in the refrigerator for up to 3-4 days.
- Customize the salad by adding your favorite vegetables or protein options.
- Serve the tabbouleh salad as a filling for wraps or pitas, or alongside grilled meats or fish.

Enjoy this vibrant and flavorful quinoa tabbouleh salad as a healthy and satisfying addition to your meal rotation. It's perfect for picnics, potlucks, or as a light lunch option! Adjust the ingredients to your liking and make it your own.

Turkey Chili with Beans

Ingredients:

- 1 tablespoon olive oil
- 1 onion, chopped
- 3 cloves garlic, minced
- 1 red bell pepper, chopped
- 1 green bell pepper, chopped
- 1 jalapeño pepper, seeded and finely chopped (optional, for heat)
- 1 pound ground turkey (lean)
- 2 tablespoons chili powder
- 1 teaspoon ground cumin
- 1 teaspoon paprika
- 1/2 teaspoon dried oregano
- 1/2 teaspoon salt, or more to taste
- 1/4 teaspoon black pepper
- 1 can (14 oz) diced tomatoes
- 1 can (15 oz) kidney beans, drained and rinsed
- 1 can (15 oz) black beans, drained and rinsed
- 2 cups chicken or vegetable broth
- Optional toppings: chopped fresh cilantro, sliced green onions, shredded cheese, sour cream, diced avocado

Instructions:

1. Sauté the Vegetables:
    - Heat olive oil in a large pot or Dutch oven over medium heat.
    - Add chopped onion, minced garlic, and chopped bell peppers (red, green) to the pot.
    - Sauté for 5-6 minutes, or until the vegetables start to soften.
2. Cook the Turkey:
    - Add ground turkey to the pot.
    - Cook, breaking up the meat with a spoon, until the turkey is browned and cooked through.
3. Season the Chili:
    - Stir in chili powder, ground cumin, paprika, dried oregano, salt, and black pepper. Cook for 1-2 minutes, stirring constantly, to toast the spices.
4. Add Tomatoes and Beans:

- Add diced tomatoes (with their juices), kidney beans, and black beans to the pot.
- Pour in the chicken or vegetable broth.
- Stir well to combine all ingredients.
5. Simmer the Chili:
    - Bring the chili to a simmer.
    - Reduce heat to low, cover the pot with a lid, and let it simmer for 20-25 minutes, stirring occasionally, to allow the flavors to meld together and the chili to thicken.
6. Adjust Seasoning and Serve:
    - Taste the chili and adjust seasoning with more salt or spices if needed.
    - Serve the turkey chili hot, garnished with chopped fresh cilantro, sliced green onions, shredded cheese, sour cream, and diced avocado if desired.

Tips for Serving:

- Customize the chili by adding other vegetables such as corn or diced carrots.
- For extra heat, leave the seeds in the jalapeño pepper or add a pinch of cayenne pepper.
- This turkey chili can be made ahead of time and stored in the refrigerator for up to 3-4 days, or frozen for longer storage.
- Serve the chili with cornbread, tortilla chips, or over rice for a complete meal.

Enjoy this flavorful and comforting turkey chili with beans as a satisfying dinner option.

It's easy to make and perfect for feeding a crowd or meal prepping for busy weekdays!

Adjust the ingredients and spices to your taste preferences and make it your own.

Ratatouille

Ingredients:

- 1 large eggplant, diced into 1-inch cubes
- 2 zucchini, diced into 1-inch cubes
- 1 yellow bell pepper, diced
- 1 red bell pepper, diced
- 1 onion, diced
- 3-4 cloves garlic, minced
- 4 ripe tomatoes, diced (or 1 can diced tomatoes)
- 2 tablespoons tomato paste
- 2 tablespoons olive oil
- 1 teaspoon dried thyme
- 1 teaspoon dried oregano
- Salt and pepper, to taste
- Fresh basil leaves, chopped, for garnish

Instructions:

1. Prepare the Vegetables:
    - Dice the eggplant, zucchini, bell peppers, and onion into 1-inch cubes or similar-sized pieces.
2. Sauté the Vegetables:
    - In a large skillet or Dutch oven, heat olive oil over medium heat.
    - Add the diced onion and garlic to the pan. Sauté for 2-3 minutes until the onion becomes translucent.
3. Cook the Eggplant and Zucchini:
    - Add the diced eggplant and zucchini to the skillet.
    - Cook for about 5-7 minutes, stirring occasionally, until the vegetables start to soften.
4. Add Bell Peppers and Tomatoes:
    - Add the diced bell peppers and tomatoes to the skillet.
    - Stir in the tomato paste, dried thyme, dried oregano, salt, and pepper.
5. Simmer the Ratatouille:
    - Reduce the heat to medium-low and let the ratatouille simmer for 20-25 minutes, or until all the vegetables are tender and the flavors have melded together. Stir occasionally.
6. Adjust Seasoning and Serve:
    - Taste and adjust seasoning with more salt and pepper if needed.

- Garnish the ratatouille with chopped fresh basil leaves before serving.

Tips for Serving Ratatouille:

- Ratatouille can be served warm or at room temperature.
- Enjoy ratatouille as a side dish, over cooked pasta, quinoa, or rice, or as a topping for toasted bread.
- This dish is even better the next day, so consider making it ahead of time and letting the flavors develop overnight.
- Ratatouille pairs well with crusty bread, a sprinkle of Parmesan cheese, or a dollop of creamy goat cheese.

Ratatouille is a delightful dish that celebrates the flavors of seasonal vegetables. It's perfect for using up an abundance of garden produce or for a simple and healthy weeknight meal. Enjoy the vibrant colors and delicious flavors of this classic French vegetable stew!

Coconut Lime Chicken Skewers

Ingredients:

- 1.5 pounds boneless, skinless chicken breasts or thighs, cut into cubes
- 1 can (13.5 oz) full-fat coconut milk
- Zest and juice of 2 limes
- 3 cloves garlic, minced
- 1 tablespoon grated fresh ginger
- 2 tablespoons soy sauce (or tamari for gluten-free)
- 1 tablespoon honey or maple syrup
- 1 teaspoon ground cumin
- 1/2 teaspoon ground coriander
- 1/2 teaspoon turmeric powder
- Salt and pepper, to taste
- Wooden or metal skewers, soaked in water if using wooden

Instructions:

1. Prepare the Marinade:
    - In a bowl, combine the coconut milk, lime zest, lime juice, minced garlic, grated ginger, soy sauce, honey or maple syrup, ground cumin, ground coriander, turmeric powder, salt, and pepper. Mix well to combine.
2. Marinate the Chicken:
    - Place the cubed chicken pieces in a shallow dish or resealable plastic bag.
    - Pour the marinade over the chicken, making sure all pieces are well coated.
    - Cover the dish or seal the bag, and refrigerate for at least 2 hours (or overnight) to allow the flavors to meld together.
3. Skewer the Chicken:
    - Preheat your grill or grill pan over medium-high heat.
    - Thread the marinated chicken pieces onto the skewers, leaving a bit of space between each piece.
4. Grill the Chicken Skewers:
    - Brush the grill grates with oil to prevent sticking.
    - Place the chicken skewers on the preheated grill.
    - Grill for 10-12 minutes, turning occasionally, until the chicken is cooked through and has nice grill marks on all sides.
5. Serve the Coconut Lime Chicken Skewers:
    - Transfer the grilled chicken skewers to a serving platter.

- Garnish with additional lime wedges and chopped fresh cilantro or parsley, if desired.
- Serve the coconut lime chicken skewers hot, alongside rice or salad.

Tips for Serving:

- Serve the coconut lime chicken skewers with a side of coconut rice, jasmine rice, or a fresh salad for a complete meal.
- Drizzle any remaining marinade over the cooked chicken skewers for extra flavor.
- If using wooden skewers, soak them in water for at least 30 minutes before threading the chicken to prevent them from burning on the grill.
- Customize the marinade by adding a dash of chili flakes or Sriracha for some heat.

Enjoy these flavorful and juicy coconut lime chicken skewers as a tasty main dish for your next barbecue or summer gathering. The marinade infuses the chicken with tropical flavors that are sure to please everyone at the table!

Cucumber Noodle Salad with Peanut Dressing

Ingredients:

For the Salad:

- 2 large English cucumbers
- 1 red bell pepper, thinly sliced
- 1 carrot, peeled and julienned
- 1/4 cup chopped fresh cilantro
- 1/4 cup chopped roasted peanuts
- Optional: cooked protein such as grilled chicken, tofu, or shrimp

For the Peanut Dressing:

- 1/4 cup creamy peanut butter
- 2 tablespoons soy sauce (or tamari for gluten-free)
- 2 tablespoons rice vinegar
- 1 tablespoon sesame oil
- 1 tablespoon honey or maple syrup
- 1 clove garlic, minced
- 1 teaspoon grated fresh ginger
- 2-3 tablespoons water, to thin the dressing
- Optional: Sriracha or chili flakes, to taste

Instructions:

1. Prepare the Cucumber Noodles:
   - Use a spiralizer or julienne peeler to create cucumber noodles from the English cucumbers. Alternatively, you can thinly slice the cucumbers lengthwise into long strips.
   - Place the cucumber noodles in a large mixing bowl.
2. Add Vegetables and Herbs:
   - Add thinly sliced red bell pepper, julienned carrot, and chopped fresh cilantro to the bowl with the cucumber noodles.
   - Toss everything together gently to combine.
3. Make the Peanut Dressing:

- In a small bowl, whisk together creamy peanut butter, soy sauce, rice vinegar, sesame oil, honey or maple syrup, minced garlic, and grated ginger.
- Add 2-3 tablespoons of water to the dressing to thin it to your desired consistency. Whisk until smooth and creamy.
- Taste the dressing and adjust seasoning. For a spicy kick, add Sriracha or chili flakes to taste.

4. Assemble the Salad:
   - Pour the peanut dressing over the cucumber noodle mixture.
   - Toss the salad gently to coat the vegetables evenly with the dressing.
5. Serve the Salad:
   - Transfer the cucumber noodle salad to serving plates or bowls.
   - Garnish with chopped roasted peanuts and additional cilantro.
   - If desired, add cooked protein such as grilled chicken, tofu, or shrimp on top of the salad.

Tips for Serving:

- This cucumber noodle salad with peanut dressing is best served immediately after assembling. However, you can prepare the components ahead of time and assemble just before serving to keep the salad crisp.
- Customize the salad by adding other vegetables such as shredded cabbage, sliced radishes, or snap peas.
- Adjust the sweetness and saltiness of the peanut dressing to suit your taste preferences.
- Serve the salad as a light lunch or dinner, or as a side dish alongside grilled meats or seafood.

Enjoy this vibrant and flavorful cucumber noodle salad with peanut dressing for a refreshing and satisfying meal! It's a great way to incorporate more vegetables into your diet and indulge in a delicious homemade dressing.

Spinach and Mushroom Quiche with Almond Flour Crust

Ingredients:

For the Almond Flour Crust:

- 1 1/2 cups almond flour
- 1/4 teaspoon salt
- 1/4 teaspoon garlic powder (optional)
- 1/4 cup melted butter or olive oil
- 1 egg

For the Spinach and Mushroom Filling:

- 1 tablespoon olive oil
- 8 oz (225g) mushrooms, sliced (cremini or button mushrooms work well)
- 2 cups fresh spinach, roughly chopped
- 1 small onion, finely chopped
- 3 cloves garlic, minced
- Salt and pepper, to taste
- 4 large eggs
- 1/2 cup milk or cream (dairy or non-dairy)
- 1/2 cup shredded cheese (such as Gruyere, Swiss, or cheddar)
- 1/4 teaspoon ground nutmeg (optional)
- Fresh parsley or chives, chopped (for garnish)

Instructions:

1. Make the Almond Flour Crust:

- Preheat your oven to 350°F (175°C).
- In a mixing bowl, combine the almond flour, salt, and garlic powder (if using).
- Add the melted butter or olive oil and the egg to the almond flour mixture.
- Mix until a dough forms and everything is well combined.
- Press the dough evenly into a 9-inch tart or pie pan, covering the bottom and sides.
- Use a fork to prick the crust a few times to prevent air bubbles.
- Bake the crust in the preheated oven for 10-12 minutes, until lightly golden. Remove from the oven and set aside.

2. Prepare the Spinach and Mushroom Filling:

    - In a skillet, heat olive oil over medium heat.
    - Add the chopped onion and minced garlic, sautéing until softened and fragrant.
    - Add the sliced mushrooms to the skillet and cook until they release their moisture and start to brown.
    - Stir in the chopped spinach and cook for a few more minutes until the spinach wilts.
    - Season the filling with salt and pepper to taste. Remove from heat and set aside to cool slightly.

3. Assemble the Quiche:

    - In a mixing bowl, whisk together the eggs and milk or cream.
    - Stir in the shredded cheese and ground nutmeg (if using).
    - Spread the spinach and mushroom filling evenly over the pre-baked almond flour crust.
    - Pour the egg and cheese mixture over the filling, making sure it's evenly distributed.
    - Gently tap the pan on the counter to release any air bubbles.

4. Bake the Quiche:

    - Place the quiche in the preheated oven and bake for 25-30 minutes, or until the center is set and the top is golden brown.
    - Remove from the oven and let the quiche cool for 10-15 minutes before slicing.
    - Garnish with fresh chopped parsley or chives before serving.

5. Serve and Enjoy:

    - Slice the spinach and mushroom quiche into wedges.
    - Serve warm or at room temperature as a delicious and satisfying meal.

Tips for Serving:

    - This spinach and mushroom quiche is versatile and can be served for brunch, lunch, or dinner.

- Feel free to customize the filling with other vegetables or add cooked bacon or ham for extra flavor.
- Store any leftover quiche in the refrigerator for up to 3-4 days. Reheat slices in the microwave or oven before serving.

Enjoy this delightful spinach and mushroom quiche with an almond flour crust for a flavorful and satisfying dish that's perfect for any occasion!

Baked Acorn Squash with Wild Rice Stuffing

Ingredients:

For the Acorn Squash:

- 2 medium acorn squash
- 2 tablespoons olive oil
- Salt and pepper, to taste

For the Wild Rice Stuffing:

- 1 cup wild rice, rinsed
- 2 1/2 cups vegetable or chicken broth
- 1 tablespoon olive oil
- 1 onion, finely chopped
- 2 cloves garlic, minced
- 2 celery stalks, finely chopped
- 1 carrot, finely chopped
- 1/2 cup dried cranberries or chopped dried apricots
- 1/2 cup pecans or walnuts, chopped
- 2 tablespoons chopped fresh parsley
- 1 tablespoon chopped fresh sage (or 1 teaspoon dried sage)
- Salt and pepper, to taste

Instructions:

1. Prepare the Acorn Squash:

- Preheat your oven to 400°F (200°C).
- Wash the acorn squash and slice them in half lengthwise.
- Scoop out the seeds and stringy pulp from each half using a spoon.
- Brush the cut sides of the squash halves with olive oil and season with salt and pepper.
- Place the squash halves cut-side down on a baking sheet lined with parchment paper.
- Roast in the preheated oven for 25-30 minutes, or until the squash is tender when pierced with a fork.

2. Cook the Wild Rice:

- In a saucepan, combine the rinsed wild rice and vegetable or chicken broth.
- Bring to a boil over high heat, then reduce the heat to low and cover.
- Simmer for 40-45 minutes, or until the wild rice is tender and has absorbed all the liquid.
- Drain any excess liquid and set the cooked wild rice aside.

3. Make the Wild Rice Stuffing:

- In a large skillet, heat olive oil over medium heat.
- Add the chopped onion, garlic, celery, and carrot to the skillet.
- Sauté for 5-7 minutes, or until the vegetables are softened.
- Stir in the cooked wild rice, dried cranberries or chopped dried apricots, chopped pecans or walnuts, chopped fresh parsley, and chopped fresh sage.
- Season the stuffing mixture with salt and pepper to taste.
- Cook for another 2-3 minutes to allow the flavors to meld together.
- Remove from heat.

4. Assemble and Bake:

- Preheat your oven to 375°F (190°C).
- Flip the roasted acorn squash halves over on the baking sheet, cut-side up.
- Spoon the wild rice stuffing mixture into each acorn squash half, pressing gently to fill the cavity.

5. Bake the Stuffed Squash:

- Place the stuffed acorn squash halves back in the oven.
- Bake for an additional 15-20 minutes, or until the stuffing is heated through and the tops are lightly browned.

6. Serve and Enjoy:

- Remove the stuffed acorn squash from the oven and let them cool slightly.
- Serve the baked acorn squash with wild rice stuffing as a delicious and festive main dish or side.

Tips for Serving:

- Garnish the stuffed acorn squash with additional fresh herbs, such as parsley or sage, before serving.

- Add crumbled goat cheese or feta on top of the stuffing for extra creaminess and flavor.
- This dish can be prepared ahead of time. Assemble the stuffed squash and refrigerate until ready to bake, then bake just before serving.

Enjoy this comforting and flavorful baked acorn squash with wild rice stuffing for a wholesome and satisfying meal that's perfect for autumn or winter gatherings!

Lemon Herb Grilled Shrimp Skewers

Ingredients:

- 1 pound large shrimp, peeled and deveined
- Zest and juice of 2 lemons
- 3 cloves garlic, minced
- 2 tablespoons chopped fresh parsley
- 2 tablespoons chopped fresh basil
- 1 tablespoon chopped fresh dill (or 1 teaspoon dried dill)
- 1/4 cup olive oil
- Salt and pepper, to taste
- Wooden or metal skewers, soaked in water if using wooden

Instructions:

1. Prepare the Marinade:
- In a bowl, combine the lemon zest, lemon juice, minced garlic, chopped parsley, chopped basil, chopped dill, olive oil, salt, and pepper. Mix well to combine.
2. Marinate the Shrimp:
- Place the peeled and deveined shrimp in a shallow dish or resealable plastic bag.
- Pour the marinade over the shrimp, making sure all shrimp are coated evenly.
- Cover the dish or seal the bag, and refrigerate for at least 30 minutes to allow the flavors to meld together. You can marinate the shrimp for up to 2 hours.
3. Skewer the Shrimp:
- Preheat your grill or grill pan over medium-high heat.
- Thread the marinated shrimp onto skewers, dividing evenly and leaving a little space between each shrimp.
4. Grill the Shrimp Skewers:
- Brush the grill grates with a bit of oil to prevent sticking.
- Place the shrimp skewers on the preheated grill.
- Grill for 2-3 minutes per side, or until the shrimp turn pink and opaque. Be careful not to overcook the shrimp, as they can become tough.
5. Serve and Enjoy:
- Remove the grilled shrimp skewers from the grill and transfer them to a serving platter.
- Garnish with additional chopped fresh herbs and lemon wedges if desired.
- Serve the lemon herb grilled shrimp skewers hot, as a main dish or as part of a seafood platter.

Tips for Serving:

- Serve the grilled shrimp skewers with a side of rice, couscous, or a fresh green salad.
- These shrimp skewers are great for entertaining! Serve them at summer barbecues, parties, or gatherings.
- Feel free to customize the marinade by adding a pinch of red pepper flakes for a hint of spice or swapping out the herbs based on your preference.
- You can also grill some vegetables alongside the shrimp skewers, such as bell peppers, zucchini, or cherry tomatoes, for a complete meal.

Enjoy these flavorful and juicy lemon herb grilled shrimp skewers for a delicious and easy-to-make dish that's perfect for any occasion. They're sure to be a hit with family and friends!

Black Bean and Sweet Potato Tacos

Ingredients:

For the Sweet Potatoes:

- 2 medium sweet potatoes, peeled and diced into small cubes
- 2 tablespoons olive oil
- 1 teaspoon ground cumin
- 1 teaspoon chili powder
- Salt and pepper, to taste

For the Black Beans:

- 1 can (15 oz) black beans, drained and rinsed
- 1 clove garlic, minced
- 1/2 teaspoon ground cumin
- 1/2 teaspoon chili powder
- Salt and pepper, to taste
- Juice of 1 lime

For Assembling Tacos:

- Corn or flour tortillas
- Toppings: sliced avocado or guacamole, diced red onion, chopped fresh cilantro, crumbled feta or cotija cheese, salsa or hot sauce, lime wedges

Instructions:

1. Roast the Sweet Potatoes:

- Preheat your oven to 400°F (200°C).
- In a large bowl, toss the diced sweet potatoes with olive oil, ground cumin, chili powder, salt, and pepper until evenly coated.
- Spread the sweet potatoes in a single layer on a baking sheet.
- Roast in the preheated oven for 20-25 minutes, or until the sweet potatoes are tender and lightly browned, stirring halfway through.

2. Prepare the Black Beans:

- In a saucepan, heat a tablespoon of olive oil over medium heat.

- Add the minced garlic and sauté for about 30 seconds, until fragrant.
- Add the drained and rinsed black beans, ground cumin, chili powder, salt, pepper, and lime juice.
- Cook for 5-7 minutes, stirring occasionally, until the beans are heated through and well seasoned.

3. Assemble the Tacos:

- Warm the tortillas in a dry skillet or microwave.
- Spoon some of the black beans onto each tortilla.
- Top with a generous portion of roasted sweet potatoes.
- Add your favorite toppings such as sliced avocado or guacamole, diced red onion, chopped fresh cilantro, crumbled feta or cotija cheese, salsa or hot sauce, and a squeeze of lime juice.

4. Serve and Enjoy:

- Serve the black bean and sweet potato tacos immediately.
- Enjoy these delicious vegetarian tacos as a tasty and satisfying meal.

Tips for Serving:

- Customize the tacos with additional toppings like shredded lettuce, diced tomatoes, or pickled jalapeños.
- Make it vegan by omitting the cheese or using a dairy-free alternative.
- These tacos are great for meal prep! Prepare the sweet potatoes and black beans ahead of time and assemble the tacos when ready to eat.
- Serve with a side of Mexican rice, refried beans, or a simple salad for a complete meal.

These black bean and sweet potato tacos are a flavorful and wholesome dish that's sure to be a hit with your family or guests. They're packed with protein, fiber, and delicious flavors, making them a perfect choice for a meatless dinner option!

Tomato Basil Zucchini Noodles

Ingredients:

- 4 medium zucchini
- 2 tablespoons olive oil
- 3 cloves garlic, minced
- 2 cups cherry or grape tomatoes, halved
- Salt and pepper, to taste
- 1/4 teaspoon red pepper flakes (optional)
- 1/4 cup chopped fresh basil leaves
- Grated Parmesan cheese, for serving (optional)

Instructions:

1. Prepare the Zucchini Noodles:

- Using a spiralizer, julienne peeler, or vegetable peeler, create zucchini noodles (zoodles) by cutting the zucchini into thin, noodle-like strips. Set aside.

2. Cook the Tomato Basil Sauce:

- In a large skillet, heat olive oil over medium heat.
- Add minced garlic to the skillet and sauté for about 30 seconds, until fragrant.
- Add the halved cherry tomatoes to the skillet.
- Season with salt, pepper, and red pepper flakes (if using).
- Cook for 5-7 minutes, stirring occasionally, until the tomatoes start to soften and release their juices.

3. Add the Zucchini Noodles:

- Add the zucchini noodles to the skillet with the tomato mixture.
- Toss the noodles with the tomatoes and garlic, ensuring they are coated in the sauce.
- Cook for 2-3 minutes, stirring gently, until the zucchini noodles are just tender but still have a slight crunch.

4. Finish and Serve:

- Remove the skillet from heat.

- Stir in the chopped fresh basil leaves, reserving some for garnish.
- Taste and adjust seasoning if needed.

5. Serve the Tomato Basil Zucchini Noodles:

- Divide the zucchini noodles among serving plates.
- Garnish with additional chopped basil leaves and grated Parmesan cheese, if desired.
- Serve immediately as a light and healthy meal.

Tips for Serving:

- Feel free to customize this dish by adding protein such as grilled chicken, shrimp, or chickpeas for added substance.
- Substitute or add other vegetables like spinach, bell peppers, or mushrooms to the sauce for extra flavor and nutrients.
- For a vegan version, skip the Parmesan cheese or use a dairy-free alternative.

Enjoy these fresh and flavorful tomato basil zucchini noodles as a nutritious and satisfying meal. They're perfect for summer when zucchini is in season, but you can enjoy this dish any time of the year for a light and tasty dinner option!

Greek Chicken Souvlaki Bowls

Ingredients:

For the Chicken Souvlaki:

- 1.5 pounds boneless, skinless chicken breasts or thighs, cut into bite-sized pieces
- 1/4 cup olive oil
- Juice of 1 lemon
- 3 cloves garlic, minced
- 1 teaspoon dried oregano
- 1 teaspoon dried thyme
- 1/2 teaspoon paprika
- Salt and pepper, to taste

For the Bowls:

- Cooked quinoa or rice
- Cherry tomatoes, halved
- Cucumber, diced
- Red onion, thinly sliced
- Kalamata olives, pitted and sliced
- Feta cheese, crumbled
- Tzatziki sauce (store-bought or homemade)
- Fresh parsley or dill, chopped, for garnish
- Lemon wedges, for serving

Instructions:

1. Marinate the Chicken:

- In a bowl, whisk together the olive oil, lemon juice, minced garlic, dried oregano, dried thyme, paprika, salt, and pepper.
- Add the chicken pieces to the marinade, tossing to coat.
- Cover and refrigerate for at least 30 minutes, or ideally up to 2 hours for best flavor.

2. Cook the Chicken:

- Preheat a grill pan or skillet over medium-high heat.
- Thread the marinated chicken pieces onto skewers if using.
- Cook the chicken skewers for 5-7 minutes per side, or until the chicken is cooked through and nicely charred. Alternatively, you can cook the chicken directly in the skillet.

3. Assemble the Bowls:

- Prepare cooked quinoa or rice according to package instructions.
- Divide the cooked quinoa or rice among serving bowls.
- Top each bowl with cooked chicken souvlaki skewers or pieces.

4. Add Toppings:

- Arrange cherry tomatoes, diced cucumber, thinly sliced red onion, sliced Kalamata olives, and crumbled feta cheese over the quinoa or rice.

5. Serve with Tzatziki Sauce:

- Drizzle each bowl with tzatziki sauce.
- Garnish with chopped fresh parsley or dill.
- Serve the Greek chicken souvlaki bowls with lemon wedges on the side.

Tips for Serving:

- Customize the bowls with additional toppings such as sliced bell peppers, artichoke hearts, or roasted red peppers.
- Make a batch of homemade tzatziki sauce by combining Greek yogurt, grated cucumber, minced garlic, lemon juice, dill, salt, and pepper.
- These bowls can be meal-prepped by cooking the chicken and quinoa or rice ahead of time. Assemble the bowls when ready to eat for a quick and convenient meal.

Enjoy these Greek chicken souvlaki bowls packed with Mediterranean flavors and fresh ingredients. They're a delicious and satisfying dish that's sure to become a favorite for lunch or dinner!

Cauliflower Pizza Crust with Veggie Toppings

Ingredients:

For the Cauliflower Pizza Crust:

- 1 medium head of cauliflower, cut into florets
- 1/2 cup shredded mozzarella cheese
- 1/4 cup grated Parmesan cheese
- 1 egg
- 1 teaspoon dried oregano
- 1/2 teaspoon garlic powder
- Salt and pepper, to taste

For the Veggie Toppings:

- 1/2 cup pizza sauce or marinara sauce
- Your favorite vegetables for toppings (e.g., sliced bell peppers, cherry tomatoes, red onion, mushrooms, spinach, olives, etc.)
- Additional shredded mozzarella cheese, for topping
- Fresh basil leaves, chopped, for garnish

Instructions:

1. Prepare the Cauliflower Crust:

- Preheat your oven to 400°F (200°C).
- Place the cauliflower florets in a food processor and pulse until finely chopped and resembling rice.
- Transfer the cauliflower rice to a microwave-safe bowl and microwave on high for 4-5 minutes, or until softened.
- Let the cauliflower rice cool slightly, then place it in a clean kitchen towel or cheesecloth. Squeeze out as much moisture as possible from the cauliflower.

2. Make the Pizza Crust:

- In a bowl, combine the squeezed cauliflower rice, shredded mozzarella cheese, grated Parmesan cheese, egg, dried oregano, garlic powder, salt, and pepper. Mix well to form a dough-like consistency.
- Line a baking sheet with parchment paper and lightly grease it with olive oil or cooking spray.
- Place the cauliflower dough on the baking sheet and use your hands to flatten and shape it into a round pizza crust, about 1/4 inch thick.
- Bake the crust in the preheated oven for 20-25 minutes, or until golden and crispy around the edges.

3. Assemble the Pizza:

- Remove the cauliflower pizza crust from the oven and spread pizza sauce or marinara sauce evenly over the crust.
- Top the sauce with your favorite vegetables for toppings, such as sliced bell peppers, cherry tomatoes, red onion, mushrooms, spinach, olives, etc.
- Sprinkle additional shredded mozzarella cheese over the toppings.

4. Bake the Pizza:

- Return the assembled pizza to the oven and bake for an additional 10-12 minutes, or until the cheese is melted and bubbly.

5. Serve and Enjoy:

- Remove the cauliflower pizza from the oven and let it cool slightly.
- Garnish with chopped fresh basil leaves.
- Slice and serve the cauliflower pizza crust with veggie toppings while warm.

Tips for Serving:

- Feel free to customize the toppings based on your preferences. You can add cooked chicken, pepperoni, or other proteins if desired.
- Make sure to thoroughly squeeze out the moisture from the cauliflower rice to prevent a soggy crust.
- Leftover cauliflower pizza can be stored in an airtight container in the refrigerator for up to 2-3 days. Reheat slices in the oven or microwave before serving.

Enjoy this cauliflower pizza crust with veggie toppings as a healthy and delicious alternative to traditional pizza. It's a great way to sneak in extra vegetables and satisfy your pizza cravings without the guilt!

Roasted Beet and Arugula Salad

Ingredients:

For the Roasted Beets:

- 3 medium beets, trimmed and scrubbed
- 2 tablespoons olive oil
- Salt and pepper, to taste

For the Salad:

- 4 cups baby arugula
- 1/4 cup crumbled goat cheese or feta cheese
- 1/4 cup chopped walnuts, toasted
- Balsamic vinaigrette (store-bought or homemade)

For the Balsamic Vinaigrette:

- 1/4 cup balsamic vinegar
- 1/2 cup extra virgin olive oil
- 1 tablespoon Dijon mustard
- 1 clove garlic, minced
- Salt and pepper, to taste

Instructions:

1. Roast the Beets:

- Preheat your oven to 400°F (200°C).
- Place the trimmed and scrubbed beets on a large piece of aluminum foil.
- Drizzle with olive oil and season with salt and pepper.
- Wrap the beets tightly in the foil and place on a baking sheet.
- Roast in the preheated oven for 45-60 minutes, or until the beets are tender when pierced with a fork.
- Let the roasted beets cool slightly, then peel off the skins (they should come off easily). Cut the beets into wedges or cubes.

2. Make the Balsamic Vinaigrette:

- In a small bowl or jar, whisk together the balsamic vinegar, extra virgin olive oil, Dijon mustard, minced garlic, salt, and pepper until well combined. Alternatively, you can shake the ingredients together in a sealed jar.

3. Assemble the Salad:

- In a large salad bowl, combine the baby arugula and roasted beet wedges or cubes.
- Drizzle with the prepared balsamic vinaigrette and toss gently to coat the salad evenly with dressing.
- Sprinkle crumbled goat cheese (or feta cheese) and chopped toasted walnuts over the salad.

4. Serve and Enjoy:

- Divide the roasted beet and arugula salad among serving plates.
- Serve immediately as a delicious and vibrant salad.

Tips for Serving:

- Feel free to add other ingredients to the salad such as sliced red onion, avocado slices, or cooked quinoa for added texture and flavor.
- Toast the walnuts in a dry skillet over medium heat for 3-4 minutes, stirring frequently, until fragrant and lightly golden.
- This salad can be served as a side dish or a light main course. Pair it with grilled chicken, salmon, or crusty bread for a complete meal.
- Prepare the roasted beets and balsamic vinaigrette ahead of time to save on prep time when assembling the salad.

Enjoy this roasted beet and arugula salad with its delightful mix of flavors and textures.

It's perfect for a healthy lunch, dinner, or as a side dish for special occasions!

Teriyaki Salmon with Steamed Broccoli

Ingredients:

For the Teriyaki Salmon:

- 4 salmon fillets (about 6 oz each), skinless
- 1/4 cup soy sauce (or tamari for gluten-free)
- 2 tablespoons honey or maple syrup
- 2 tablespoons rice vinegar
- 1 tablespoon sesame oil
- 2 cloves garlic, minced
- 1 teaspoon grated fresh ginger
- 1 tablespoon cornstarch (optional, for thickening the sauce)
- Sesame seeds, for garnish (optional)
- Sliced green onions, for garnish (optional)

For the Steamed Broccoli:

- 1 large head of broccoli, cut into florets
- Salt, to taste

Instructions:

1. Marinate the Salmon:

- In a bowl, whisk together soy sauce (or tamari), honey or maple syrup, rice vinegar, sesame oil, minced garlic, and grated ginger to make the teriyaki marinade.
- Place the salmon fillets in a shallow dish or resealable plastic bag. Pour half of the teriyaki marinade over the salmon, reserving the other half for later. Marinate the salmon for at least 30 minutes, or up to 1 hour in the refrigerator.

2. Prepare the Teriyaki Sauce:

- If you prefer a thicker sauce, whisk 1 tablespoon of cornstarch with 1 tablespoon of water in a small bowl until smooth. Set aside.
- In a small saucepan, bring the reserved teriyaki marinade to a simmer over medium heat.

- Once simmering, add the cornstarch mixture (if using) to the saucepan, stirring constantly until the sauce thickens slightly.
- Remove from heat and set aside.

3. Cook the Salmon:

- Preheat your oven to 400°F (200°C).
- Place the marinated salmon fillets on a baking sheet lined with parchment paper or foil.
- Bake in the preheated oven for 12-15 minutes, or until the salmon is cooked to your desired doneness and flakes easily with a fork.

4. Steam the Broccoli:

- While the salmon is baking, steam the broccoli florets. Fill a pot with a few inches of water and bring to a boil.
- Place the broccoli florets in a steamer basket or colander set over the boiling water. Cover and steam for 4-5 minutes, or until the broccoli is tender-crisp. Avoid overcooking to retain the bright green color and crunchiness.

5. Assemble the Dish:

- Divide the steamed broccoli among serving plates.
- Place a baked teriyaki salmon fillet on top of each serving of broccoli.
- Drizzle the thickened teriyaki sauce over the salmon fillets.
- Garnish with sesame seeds and sliced green onions, if desired.

6. Serve and Enjoy:

- Serve the teriyaki salmon with steamed broccoli immediately.
- Enjoy this delicious and healthy dish as a satisfying meal.

Tips for Serving:

- Serve the teriyaki salmon and steamed broccoli with cooked rice or quinoa for a complete meal.
- Customize the dish by adding additional vegetables such as sliced bell peppers, snap peas, or carrots.
- Double the teriyaki marinade recipe if you prefer extra sauce for serving or dipping.

- Store any leftovers in an airtight container in the refrigerator for up to 2-3 days.

This teriyaki salmon with steamed broccoli is a flavorful and nutritious dish that's perfect for weeknight dinners or special occasions. Enjoy the tender salmon and vibrant broccoli with the delicious homemade teriyaki sauce!

Moroccan Spiced Chickpea Stew

Ingredients:

- 2 tablespoons olive oil
- 1 onion, finely chopped
- 3 cloves garlic, minced
- 1 teaspoon ground cumin
- 1 teaspoon ground coriander
- 1 teaspoon ground turmeric
- 1/2 teaspoon ground cinnamon
- 1/2 teaspoon ground paprika
- 1/4 teaspoon cayenne pepper (adjust to taste)
- 1 can (15 oz) chickpeas, drained and rinsed (or 1 1/2 cups cooked chickpeas)
- 1 can (14.5 oz) diced tomatoes
- 3 cups vegetable broth
- 1 medium sweet potato, peeled and diced
- 1 red bell pepper, diced
- 1 zucchini, diced
- Salt and pepper, to taste
- Fresh cilantro or parsley, chopped, for garnish
- Lemon wedges, for serving
- Cooked couscous or rice, for serving (optional)

Instructions:

1. Sauté the Aromatics:

- In a large pot or Dutch oven, heat the olive oil over medium heat.
- Add the chopped onion and sauté for 5-6 minutes, or until softened and translucent.
- Stir in the minced garlic, ground cumin, ground coriander, ground turmeric, ground cinnamon, ground paprika, and cayenne pepper. Cook for 1-2 minutes, stirring constantly, until fragrant.

2. Add Chickpeas and Tomatoes:

- Add the drained and rinsed chickpeas to the pot, along with the diced tomatoes (with their juices).
- Stir to combine and cook for 2-3 minutes.

3. Simmer the Stew:

- Pour in the vegetable broth and bring the mixture to a simmer.
- Add the diced sweet potato, diced red bell pepper, and diced zucchini to the pot.
- Season with salt and pepper, to taste.

4. Cook Until Vegetables are Tender:

- Cover the pot and reduce the heat to medium-low.
- Let the stew simmer for 20-25 minutes, or until the sweet potatoes are tender and cooked through.

5. Adjust Seasoning and Serve:

- Taste the stew and adjust seasoning with additional salt, pepper, or spices if needed.
- Serve the Moroccan spiced chickpea stew hot, garnished with chopped fresh cilantro or parsley.
- Serve with lemon wedges on the side for squeezing over the stew.
- Optionally, serve the stew over cooked couscous or rice for a complete meal.

Tips for Serving:

- Customize the stew with additional vegetables such as carrots, eggplant, or spinach.
- For added protein, you can stir in cooked quinoa or lentils along with the chickpeas.
- Store any leftovers in an airtight container in the refrigerator for up to 4-5 days. The flavors will develop even more over time.
- This stew can be frozen for longer storage. Let it cool completely before transferring to freezer-safe containers or bags. Thaw overnight in the refrigerator before reheating.

Enjoy this Moroccan spiced chickpea stew as a nourishing and satisfying meal packed with warming spices and hearty vegetables. It's perfect for a cozy dinner with family or friends!

Turkey and Vegetable Skillet

Ingredients:

- 1 tablespoon olive oil
- 1 pound ground turkey (or chicken)
- 1 onion, diced
- 2 cloves garlic, minced
- 1 bell pepper, diced (any color)
- 1 zucchini, diced
- 1 cup diced tomatoes (fresh or canned)
- 1 teaspoon dried oregano
- 1 teaspoon ground cumin
- 1/2 teaspoon paprika
- Salt and pepper, to taste
- 2 cups baby spinach or kale
- Optional toppings: chopped fresh herbs (parsley or cilantro), sliced avocado, shredded cheese, hot sauce

Instructions:

1. Sauté the Turkey and Vegetables:

- Heat olive oil in a large skillet or frying pan over medium-high heat.
- Add the diced onion and cook for 2-3 minutes until softened.
- Add the minced garlic and cook for another 30 seconds until fragrant.
- Add the ground turkey to the skillet, breaking it up with a spoon or spatula. Cook until the turkey is browned and cooked through.

2. Add Vegetables and Spices:

- Stir in the diced bell pepper and zucchini. Cook for 3-4 minutes until the vegetables begin to soften.
- Add the diced tomatoes, dried oregano, ground cumin, paprika, salt, and pepper. Stir well to combine.

3. Simmer and Finish:

- Reduce the heat to medium-low and let the mixture simmer for 5-7 minutes, allowing the flavors to meld together and the vegetables to cook through.
- Taste and adjust seasoning as needed with additional salt, pepper, or spices.
- Stir in the baby spinach or kale, allowing it to wilt slightly in the skillet.

4. Serve:

- Remove the skillet from heat.
- Serve the turkey and vegetable mixture hot, garnished with optional toppings like chopped fresh herbs, sliced avocado, shredded cheese, or hot sauce.
- Enjoy the turkey and vegetable skillet as is or serve it over cooked quinoa, rice, or cauliflower rice for a complete meal.

Tips for Serving:

- Customize the vegetables based on what you have on hand or your preferences. Try adding diced carrots, broccoli florets, or mushrooms.
- Feel free to substitute ground turkey with ground chicken, beef, or plant-based ground meat.
- This skillet meal is versatile and can be enjoyed on its own or served with a side salad, crusty bread, or tortillas for wrapping.
- Store any leftovers in an airtight container in the refrigerator for up to 3-4 days. Reheat gently on the stove or in the microwave before serving.

This turkey and vegetable skillet is a nutritious and satisfying dish that's packed with protein and vegetables. It's a great option for a wholesome dinner that the whole family will love!

Eggplant and Tomato Casserole

Ingredients:

- 2 large eggplants, sliced into rounds (about 1/2-inch thick)
- Salt, for sweating eggplant
- Olive oil, for brushing eggplant slices
- 2 tablespoons olive oil
- 1 onion, finely chopped
- 3 cloves garlic, minced
- 1 can (14.5 oz) diced tomatoes, drained
- 1 can (14.5 oz) crushed tomatoes
- 1 teaspoon dried oregano
- 1 teaspoon dried basil
- Salt and pepper, to taste
- 1 cup shredded mozzarella cheese (or Parmesan cheese)
- Fresh basil leaves, chopped, for garnish

Instructions:

1. Prepare the Eggplant:

- Place the eggplant slices on a baking sheet lined with paper towels.
- Sprinkle both sides of the eggplant slices with salt and let them sit for about 20-30 minutes. This helps draw out excess moisture and bitterness from the eggplant.
- After 20-30 minutes, pat the eggplant slices dry with paper towels to remove the moisture.

2. Roast the Eggplant:

- Preheat your oven to 400°F (200°C).
- Brush both sides of the eggplant slices with olive oil.
- Arrange the eggplant slices on a baking sheet in a single layer.
- Roast in the preheated oven for about 20-25 minutes, flipping halfway through, until the eggplant slices are golden and tender. Remove from the oven and set aside.

3. Make the Tomato Sauce:

- In a large skillet or saucepan, heat 2 tablespoons of olive oil over medium heat.
- Add the chopped onion and cook for 5-6 minutes until softened and translucent.
- Add the minced garlic and cook for another 30 seconds until fragrant.
- Stir in the drained diced tomatoes and crushed tomatoes.
- Add the dried oregano, dried basil, salt, and pepper. Stir to combine.

4. Assemble the Casserole:

- In a greased baking dish (such as a 9x13-inch dish), spread a layer of the tomato sauce on the bottom.
- Arrange a layer of roasted eggplant slices on top of the sauce.
- Repeat with another layer of tomato sauce, followed by another layer of eggplant slices, until all ingredients are used, finishing with a layer of tomato sauce on top.

5. Bake the Casserole:

- Sprinkle the shredded mozzarella cheese evenly over the top of the casserole.
- Cover the baking dish with aluminum foil.
- Bake in the preheated oven for 25-30 minutes, then remove the foil and bake for an additional 10 minutes, or until the cheese is melted and bubbly.

6. Serve and Enjoy:

- Remove the eggplant and tomato casserole from the oven.
- Let it cool slightly before serving.
- Garnish with chopped fresh basil leaves.
- Serve the casserole warm as a main dish or a side dish.

Tips for Serving:

- This eggplant and tomato casserole can be served on its own or with a side of crusty bread, pasta, or a green salad.
- Feel free to customize the casserole by adding other vegetables such as sliced bell peppers or zucchini.
- Store any leftovers in an airtight container in the refrigerator for up to 3-4 days. Reheat in the oven or microwave before serving.

Enjoy this flavorful and comforting eggplant and tomato casserole as a satisfying meal that's perfect for sharing with family and friends!

Coconut Curry Vegetable Soup

Ingredients:

- 1 tablespoon coconut oil or vegetable oil
- 1 onion, diced
- 3 cloves garlic, minced
- 1 tablespoon grated fresh ginger
- 2 tablespoons red curry paste
- 1 sweet potato, peeled and diced
- 2 carrots, peeled and sliced
- 1 bell pepper (any color), diced
- 1 zucchini, diced
- 1 can (14 oz) chickpeas, drained and rinsed
- 1 can (14 oz) diced tomatoes
- 1 can (14 oz) coconut milk (full-fat for creaminess)
- 4 cups vegetable broth
- 1 tablespoon soy sauce or tamari (optional)
- 1 tablespoon brown sugar or maple syrup (optional)
- Salt and pepper, to taste
- Fresh cilantro or basil leaves, chopped, for garnish
- Lime wedges, for serving
- Cooked rice or noodles, for serving (optional)

Instructions:

1. Sauté Aromatics:

- In a large pot or Dutch oven, heat coconut oil or vegetable oil over medium heat.
- Add diced onion and sauté for 5-6 minutes until softened and translucent.
- Stir in minced garlic and grated ginger, and cook for another 1-2 minutes until fragrant.

2. Add Curry Paste and Vegetables:

- Add red curry paste to the pot and stir to coat the onions and aromatics.
- Add diced sweet potato, sliced carrots, diced bell pepper, and diced zucchini to the pot. Stir to combine with the curry paste.

3. Simmer with Broth and Coconut Milk:

- Pour in vegetable broth and coconut milk, and stir to combine.
- Bring the soup to a simmer over medium heat.
- Add drained and rinsed chickpeas and diced tomatoes to the pot.

4. Season and Simmer:

- Stir in soy sauce or tamari and brown sugar or maple syrup (if using) for additional flavor.
- Season the soup with salt and pepper, to taste.
- Reduce the heat to low, cover the pot, and let the soup simmer for 15-20 minutes, or until the vegetables are tender.

5. Serve:

- Ladle the coconut curry vegetable soup into bowls.
- Garnish with chopped fresh cilantro or basil leaves.
- Serve with lime wedges on the side for squeezing over the soup.
- Optionally, serve the soup over cooked rice or noodles for a more substantial meal.

Tips for Serving:

- Customize the vegetables based on what you have on hand or your preferences. Try adding spinach, kale, cauliflower, or peas.
- Adjust the level of spiciness by adding more or less red curry paste.
- For a protein boost, add cooked tofu, tempeh, or shredded chicken to the soup.
- Store any leftover soup in an airtight container in the refrigerator for up to 4-5 days. Reheat gently on the stove or in the microwave before serving.

Enjoy this creamy and aromatic Coconut Curry Vegetable Soup for a satisfying and nourishing meal. It's packed with flavor and perfect for cozy evenings!

Stuffed Bell Peppers with Ground Turkey and Quinoa

Ingredients:

- 4 large bell peppers (any color), tops cut off and seeds removed
- 1 tablespoon olive oil
- 1 onion, diced
- 3 cloves garlic, minced
- 1 pound ground turkey (or chicken)
- 1 cup cooked quinoa
- 1 can (14 oz) diced tomatoes, drained
- 1 teaspoon dried oregano
- 1 teaspoon dried basil
- 1/2 teaspoon paprika
- Salt and pepper, to taste
- 1 cup shredded mozzarella cheese (or your favorite cheese), divided
- Fresh parsley or basil, chopped, for garnish

Instructions:

1. Preheat the Oven:

- Preheat your oven to 375°F (190°C). Prepare a baking dish that can hold the bell peppers upright.

2. Prepare the Bell Peppers:

- Cut the tops off the bell peppers and remove the seeds and membranes from inside.
- Place the hollowed-out bell peppers upright in the baking dish. Set aside.

3. Cook the Filling:

- In a large skillet, heat olive oil over medium heat.
- Add diced onion and minced garlic, and sauté for 2-3 minutes until softened and fragrant.

4. Brown the Ground Turkey:

- Add the ground turkey to the skillet and cook, breaking it up with a spoon, until it's no longer pink.

5. Add Quinoa and Seasonings:

    - Stir in the cooked quinoa, drained diced tomatoes, dried oregano, dried basil, paprika, salt, and pepper.
    - Cook for another 2-3 minutes, allowing the flavors to meld together.

6. Assemble the Stuffed Peppers:

    - Remove the skillet from heat and stir in half of the shredded mozzarella cheese.
    - Spoon the turkey and quinoa mixture into each hollowed-out bell pepper, pressing down gently to fill completely.
    - Sprinkle the remaining shredded mozzarella cheese on top of each stuffed pepper.

7. Bake the Stuffed Peppers:

    - Cover the baking dish with foil and bake in the preheated oven for 25-30 minutes.
    - Remove the foil and bake for an additional 10-15 minutes, or until the bell peppers are tender and the cheese is melted and bubbly.

8. Serve and Enjoy:

    - Remove the stuffed bell peppers from the oven and let them cool slightly.
    - Garnish with chopped fresh parsley or basil before serving.
    - Serve the stuffed bell peppers hot as a delicious and wholesome meal.

Tips for Serving:

- Feel free to customize the filling with your favorite vegetables or spices.
- Use any color of bell peppers for variety and visual appeal.
- Store any leftover stuffed peppers in an airtight container in the refrigerator for up to 3-4 days. Reheat in the oven or microwave before serving.
- These stuffed bell peppers are great served with a side salad or steamed vegetables.

Enjoy these delicious stuffed bell peppers with ground turkey and quinoa for a flavorful and satisfying dinner! They're packed with protein, fiber, and wholesome ingredients.

www.ingramcontent.com/pod-product-compliance
Lightning Source LLC
LaVergne TN
LVHW081556060526
838201LV00054B/1926